# The Hidden Super Power of Addiction

**Eastern wisdom and western science meet lived experience in Smart-UK's celebration of the addicted brain!**

*Rachel*
*Thank you for your wonderful contribution*
*with much love*
*Sue.*
*x*

## Sue Cox

First published in the United Kingdom in 2021 by The Cloister House Press

ISBN 978-1-913460-31-0

My name is  Sue and I  am a recovered
addict . I am not sick, or broken, defective or
deprived. I don't have a "disease " or an
intellectual or moral weakness. I am just hard
wired in a different way.
That hard wiring is not something I am
ashamed of or proud of, it is just a fact.
We are all hardwired to reflect our genetic
blueprint and our individual life experiences,
and we are all unique.
There has never been anyone like you before
and there never will be again!
If we learn about our own particular wiring,
we can use it to our best advantage.
Those of us with a predisposition towards
addictions can be very powerful if we learn
how we tick.
I am not defined by my addiction, but I know
that If we can understand how it works,
regardless of how low an ebb were are
coming from, we can rise above it, take back
our "Super Power" and soar!
This is a story of transformation.

With love and thanks to everyone who has
contributed to this book

"You changed my life without even trying"
Gez, Louise,Nicholas,Sean,Patrick,
Siobhan, Daniel, Christina, Oliver,Oscar
Kim.
Everyone I have ever taught, and have
taught me
Peter S. who saved my life.

"It is the very characteristics which define the chronic addict which are, at a biological level, remnants of extraordinary capacity for achievement, which set us apart from the average human in pre-historic times .Our propensity for excess is a function of an innate survival drive, which probably enabled us to be more successful hunter gatherers and providers for our families." -

Dayamay Dunsby

# Contents

# Contents

# Contents

# Contents

## Foreword

*Eana Meng MD-PhD student at Harvard Medical School, studying History of Science*

*We're sitting in a prison in the north of England with seven young offenders, and Sue tells us, "We are all made of stardust. You are made of the same thing as the prime minister, as Albert Einstein, as Gandhi, and everyone else." The young men look at each other. "Really?" One of them asks out of disbelief.*

*"Yes," Sue replies. "And anyone can be addicted. Addicts are 'creatures of excess'. This sets us apart. Nature selected for addiction – it is was a way of survival. The hunters and gatherers who wanted more would be the ones that survived. Addiction is not a weakness. It is not an illness. It is a strength."*
*However, addiction can and does kill, Sue goes on, and shows us the damage that addiction to drugs and alcohol can do, using before and after brain scans. Some of the boys have never seen brain scans before. One of them didn't learn how to write until he came to prison. We continue a full lesson of the biology of addiction down to neurotransmitters being released into the synaptic cleft. I feel like I'm back in a biology course, and Sue doesn't leave anything out. She tells me later, "it's an insult to them to think they won't be able to understand it. If they don't understand it, it's not because they can't, it's because I haven't done a good enough job explaining it."*

*"Things like ear acupuncture or acupressure change the way of how you feel, and it helps you gain back control. It can empower you," Sue tells the boys as she starts a brief lesson in Chinese medicine, which she*

*describes as metaphors, rather than literal natural forces. She teaches
us about yin-yang and the importance of balance in the universe and in
ourselves. It is possible to retrain the brain, to find balance and redirect
the addiction towards something else. She shows a clip of Mr Miyagi
training Daniel in Karate Kid. The boys laugh when they recognize the
"wax on, wax off" scene. But they get it. They too can train to shift their
addiction elsewhere. And ear acupuncture, they're told, can help with
that.*

I visited Her Majesty's Prison (HMP) with Sue for a young
offender's wellness training program in February 2020. She was invited
to teach the young men about addiction and acupuncture by the staff.
This particular HMP holds a special place in her heart, as she has been
visiting there for many years.

The staff are exceedingly warm and grateful for Sue's work in
creating a programme to help the prisoners manage addiction – an issue
that is stigmatized and neglected, compounded with a population that
often is as well. Sue is dedicated to working with the prison population
and has trained officers, staff, and prisoners at 128 of the HMPs in the
United Kingdom during her few decades-long career working in the
field of addiction as an acupuncturist.

She founded Substance Misuse Acupuncture Register and
Training (SMART UK), a training organization for auricular
acupuncture which works with the NHS, addiction charities, mental
health services and more in the United Kingdom and abroad. Together
with her close friend and co-founder, Kim Wagner, Sue has taught the
five-point ear acupuncture protocol to over 20,000 people. The ethos of
her work is "empowerment" and "evolution," and she continually
emphasizes that her work is always for and about the patient, the person
behind the addiction.

To understand how SMART UK has created a fellowship among
more than 20,000 people worldwide, Sue's passion must be understood.

Sue, herself, is a person behind the addiction – something she always tells me that she has no shame about. Here is her story in brief – the fuller details are to come in the following pages, and well worth the reader's time and contemplation.

Adopted into a family where "alcohol was seen as the panacea for all ills," Sue began drinking at the young age of ten. It made her feel braver and less afraid, allowing her to numb herself and momentarily escape from a childhood she could only later understand as troubling.

She was taught to revere the Catholic Church, where pain was to be cherished and offered as atonement. She was guilt-ridden and made to feel that essentially "everything apart from breathing was sinful." Her greatest pain came from when a local priest sexually abused her for three years. Her mother had witnessed the abuse but refused to speak about it, telling a thirteen-year-old Sue only to pray for the priest and to continue offering it as atonement. Unable to trust anyone, Sue turned more heavily to drinking and trying any drugs she could get her hands on, hoping to change the state of her reality.

She was married at seventeen to leave home, but an immature and violent husband only led her to increase drinking. She felt profoundly hopeless but was saved by one thing: her love for her children. It was not a feeling of rock bottom, nor a moment of great tragedy that led her to seek a way out, instead, it was the realization that if she didn't "do something about this now, then there would be a tragedy in my home, that may very well involve my children."

Despite believing that she had a genetic predisposition to addiction, she felt that there was a way out of the negative effects of it. "Bizarrely, I had a feeling that somewhere deep inside me there was something worth saving," Sue recalls, "a bit like a blade of grass trying to push its way up through something as hard as concrete." One night, after hearing about Alcohol Anonymous (AA) from a neighbour, Sue decided to make a call.

This changed the course of her life, she tells me. Having always felt like an outsider, the people she met felt familiar to her. She felt connected, understood, and comfortable. Above all, it was a sense of "fellowship," that allowed her to "glimpse a wholesome future." Yet, she disagreed with certain fundamental aspects of the AA approach, believing that the dependence on notions of a higher power, defects of character, and powerlessness was outdated, harmful, and flawed. This would come to motivate her passion for advocating for and providing proper care to those living with addiction.

Sue contends a radically different understanding of addiction from many traditional ideas. She strongly believes and attests that the addict – a term she is unafraid of using – can recover, full of potential, and deeply *powerful*. There is nothing defective about differences in brain wiring and addictive behaviour – as she had reiterated to the young offenders. Instead, it was selected by nature and has allowed humans to thrive.

Yet, it can and does kill, in awful ways when the addiction is to harmful substances. Providers, people themselves, and the public must be aware of the complexities of addiction. She is adamant that treatment and care must be taken seriously and trains only those who have had experience with addiction – whether working in the field or having lived through their own personal stories. "This isn't about party tricks and fluffy magic," Sue often repeats, "this is a matter of life and death, and we must take it seriously."

Thus, as the reader will note in the following chapters, there is an insistence on research's importance. Woven throughout Sue writings is also an ethos of translation: from Chinese medicine theories to biomedical explanations, confusing expert knowledge to comprehensible explanations that are nonetheless comprehensive.

She ultimately encourages all of us to reconsider the historically static and negative connotations that "addiction" holds and instead look upon it as multidimensional. Addiction is best understood and defined by the person who experiences it. "It is always about the man in the chair," Sue reiterates.

Sue's program and training work. Though I only have known Sue for a short time and witnessed only a few of the programs she runs, it is evident that her holistic approach to addiction recovery has helped many people understand their inherent value and see hope in their lives. Efficacy in addiction recovery is a complicated notion and evades consensus in definition – what does recovery mean? How is and should recovery be measured?

Yet, despite the differing opinions, one crucial perspective Sue urges us to take into account is what the person in recovery says themselves. As she teaches, the process begins and is sustained when a person sees their self-worth and has hope for a better and healthier future. From the young offenders to the men in the HMP I visited with Sue, it was clear that this critical message of positivity was getting through to them.

Perhaps it was the comprehensive information and explanations they were given, from the Western science to the Chinese medical theories, or maybe it was the feelings of relaxation and relief the ear acupuncture or acupressure offered.

Yet, most of all, I believe, it was Sue's undeniable passion for her work and compassion for the people that have allowed so many different people living with an addiction to see their inherent value and have hope. Her dedication to evolution, continually refining her understandings and teachings, improving how she teaches, and providing cares have all been central to how her program works.

Above all, her radiant energy brings a smile to everyone's faces, even to those of the men most hardened by life in prison. Sue would never say it, but the success of her work has been by in large, due to who she is and how much she cares for each and every member of the community, the fellowship. However, the good news is that she strongly believes this work can be and is already carried out by so many others who are dedicated to providing the most comprehensive care to those living with addiction. It is a serious, difficult, and important world to navigate; Sue's guidance lies ahead.

*Eana's Harvard research is on integrative healing practices, particularly as used by marginalized communities. Her current project focuses on the use of acupuncture by 1970s American revolutionaries and modern practitioners for addiction, substance use, and pain management."*

*She also has carved a place in our hearts!*

## Chapter One
### Smart-Uk and the Addict's hidden "Super power"!

---

The moment we hear the word "addiction" all sorts of images bombard our brains, usually very negative ones.

In fact, when you picked up this book, you may have been expecting another slant about how to help the "sick" damaged" "unfortunate" "weak" people who are addicted to chemicals. Perhaps you have already formed opinions based on the vast amount of negative beliefs about addiction and addicts. This will not be that kind of book.

It is always challenging to get rid of a negative image once we have it in our brains! If you were to read about me, for example, on paper, I think I might look quite disturbing. You might quickly assume a mental "image." of me, one that might be difficult to lose! When you read that I am a 73-year-old recovered alcoholic, addict, with an eating disorder, a self-harmer who was the single mother of six children, and who was adopted, seriously sexually abused by a priest in childhood, escaped a violent marriage, and a murder attempt - you would doubtless have acquired a very worrying picture in your head! Not an image I care to foster either!

While all of that is all entirely true, of course, it is certainly not who I am these days, and so t I will attempt to give you a different view, both of me, and addiction!

Here in this book, we are going to turn that negative "image" of addicts on its head and embrace the enormous benefits to having a brain which is hard-wired in this way, and "celebrates the addictive brain!

*The addicts "Superpower"!*

Yes! I did indeed say celebrate! We want to smash some of the long-held negative perceptions about addiction, but more particularly about addicts themselves. To explain all of that, I am going to ask you to look at the "Smart-UK" journey so far. How we began, what we then thought, and how we came to an understanding we now have, and our excitement of this optimistic viewpoint.

I have been writing this book for a couple of years now, in response to many requests! I am not a writer, I am more of a "hands-on" practitioner and teacher, but there is no doubt that the "Smart-UK" stance on addiction and the journey that took us to this place ought to be told, and I guess I am the only one who can do that! I may well repeat things, but I would rather say something twice that miss it out!! So please do read beyond my writing inadequacies and see the passion beneath!

Firstly it would be good to clarify precisely what this book is, and is not about!

I am a Traditional Acupuncturist, head of the teaching organisation *Smart-UK*. Still, this book is not about acupuncture, although we will draw on some of its theories, and it has undoubtedly been a big part of our evolution, to date I have taught over 20,000 healthcare workers!

I am a recovered addict, and I feel passionately that other addicts like me should have full knowledge of their true potential, but this book is not about me, although I admit there is something of the "memoir" about it!

My colleague and friend Kim is a neuroscientist, but his study is also only part of the story, albeit a crucial one.

The "Smart UK" story is all about awareness, potential and, more than anything, Empowerment.!

We will draw on all of our accumulated experiences and skills to tell this story.

There's no doubt we will look at "addiction" a word that people sometimes find offensive, but none the less it is the correct one, and the one we shall use; This book will be more than anything a celebration of the "Addicted Brain!"

Kim and I taught together for nearly twenty-five years, and have a combined experience in the field of addiction treatment of over sixty years, both in the NHS and private practice. My own lived experience as an addict has often even been one of the "models" for our study, having been in "recovery" myself for 45 years.

What I teach now, has minimal bearing on what we taught 25 years ago, and what we now know about recovery from addiction has also changed dramatically.

These days, however, I am falling out of love with the word "Recovery" and prefer to use the name "Restoration"! "Recovery" should be a short term situation, after which "Restoration" to true potential can begin. I am passionate about "Restoration", from any problematic root, any difficulty, damage, or trauma.

Human beings, especially those who have travelled the path of addiction, have the most amazing abilities that are rarely acknowledged. It is that absolute passion for real Empowerment that drives me to keep on learning, teaching and showing the exciting possibilities of having a brain which is wired in this way.

Kim is a Dr. of Neuroscience, and so is the magical brain behind our hypotheses! He feels passionately that things should be understood and taught correctly. He rarely teaches now but is still a significant influence on my work. We have inspired each other for nearly a quarter of a century! In this book, we hope to inspire our readers further.

We think everyone must understand the true nature of addiction, especially those caught up in its wake. We want addicts especially, to understand and not be continually dependent on others who suggest they have superior knowledge.

We will use a cross-pollination of skills and theories, both Western and Chinese, to explore the human brain, the target organ of addiction, and the most potent and complex organism in the known Universe. Livers don't get addicted, neither do kidneys; it is BRAINS that get addicted. So it makes perfect sense to explore that organ!

We will also look at how genes influence our brains, why everything that happens to us makes us who we are, and so how we behave.

Then with the help of our wonderful contributors (and friends.), we will spotlight the possibilities of amazing "transformations" and Empowerment.

As you read any of our books, you will hear two voices! Kim's is the academic one; he beautifully and precisely tells us the scientific facts. Mine is somewhat more in the vernacular! I will tell you the story behind the facts. You will notice the difference, but we have always found that the two meld beautifully and are quite necessary for each other!

You can find Kim's in-depth look at neuroscience in our first book "Auricular Acupuncture and addiction" which is more of a textbook, here I want to tell it in a more basic way. I intend to keep the brain science simple, in the way that I teach it, and how I understand it, the way that Kim has taught me!

So let's begin

## Addictive Drive

Addicts are extremely driven people! It is a fact! You only need to look at the lengths they will go to, the manipulation, the "ducking and diving", the imperative to get to their "drug of choice", to see that their drive is relentless in pursuit of that goal. Seemingly hard-wired for "all or nothing" and often referred to as "creatures of excess"! they can be hellbent on chasing that which they have fallen in love, *regardless of the consequences*. Anybody who has ever worked in this field or lived with an addict is well aware of this phenomenon!

How many times have we heard addiction workers say" "If only we could channel those creative, manipulative qualities that addicts seem to have, into something more positive!"

"If only they could find a way to harness that energy and "drive". "There must be a reason for them being this way!" "If only they would put their skills into something more useful."

It is essential right from the beginning to be clear that it is NOT possible to change that fundamental wiring! That isn't a negative statement, just a reality check! I would urge people not to pursue illusions!

Instead, we are going to explore ways to harness and embrace that exceptional wiring. How amazing it can be for a person who has left behind their "drugs of choice" to divert and transform that relentless drive, and in doing so, become empowered. Releasing their "superpower" That is the challenge!

We must never lose sight of the glaring dangers, though! We know that all "Superheroes" have their vulnerabilities: Kryptonite cripples Superman, and Achilles had his heel! We should be especially mindful of how mild-mannered Dr Bruce Banner can quickly turn into the Incredible Hulk- lots of echos there! The only things I have to avoid are mood-altering chemicals!

Addiction ought never to be glamourised; it has killed far more people than have survived! But It is fashionable these days, and perhaps beneficial, to spotlight "celebrity" addicts who have been open about their addictions, and who have become great role models for many more: Elton John, Robbie Williams, Eric Clapton, Ben Affleck, Zak Efron, Anthony Hopkins, Daniel Radcliffe, Buzz Aldrin, Leonard Nimoy, Ernest Hemingway, to name a tiny number!

And some very powerful historic addicts that could not have been further away from the downtrodden image we have weaved about addicts; Alexander the Great, Sigmund Freud, Carl Marx, Charles Dickens and Winston Churchill! They are often referred to as "High functioning addicts", but they were more likely just the "lucky ones". they were quite obviously very "driven" people none the less.

When I first entered the recovery world, in Alcoholics Anonymous, it was very much frowned upon to publicise one's addiction recovery, especially if we were in the public eye, in case we tripped up, causing others to follow! That's where the "anonymous" bit comes in. We were reminded about our "egos" too, and the humility we needed to adopt!

We have moved on quite a lot since then, and we are not so prescriptive. We do these days understand the need for balance. It is so necessary to talk to each other and not to be reluctant share our strengths and experiences, and I for one am more than happy to be in the same "tribe" as Harry Potter and the man who first walked on the moon! But keeping one foot on the ground and remembering where I came from is also crucial. Balance is always essential.

### Getting to the bottom of things.

It is our continued belief that when studying or exploring anything, it is only with a thorough understanding of a condition that we can truly get to the bottom of its nature and identify correct interventions. Without that understanding, we might choose responses of little use, and miss the most effective ones. Sadly, I think this has been a mistake made by many addiction services to date.

We must not confuse "understanding" with "condoning", clearly addictive behaviour is damaging and often involves criminality, we are absolutely aware of that, and the imperative of a "tough love" approach, but if we can understand what has happened, we might then be able to turn that destructive trait on its head and harness the innate ability of the addictive brain.

It has been a constant source of frustration for me, to see the tendency to "throw anything" at a problem to see the outcome, a bit like throwing mud at a wall to see if it sticks. Wherever there is controversy over a condition, there will inevitably be controversy about its treatment! The cynic in me wonders if there isn't a "that will do" attitude towards addicted people.

It has equally been heartbreakingly confusing for many to see someone they care about struggle for years, and eventually maybe get into some kind of recovery, only to relapse and return to their using, often worse than before. They are baffled by it, and cannot understand why their love and kindness has not been enough to sustain them. It is hard to see that addicted person as being anything other than selfish and hurtful. To make sense of why that often happens, we must examine the situation correctly, to unravel the complexity of the addictive brain.

### Passion and meaning

We know that an addict who, relentless in their drive for drink or drugs, will, despite getting "clean and sober", still be as driven as in their using years. Unless they understand where that drive comes from and channel it, the addictive cycle can quickly take hold again. Remember: We cannot change that driven brain wiring, nor indeed should we necessarily want to!

So we need to find a way that we can transform that enormous drive into positive goals. Actually "positive" would not be a good enough goal for someone who has this particular brain wiring! It will have to be something bigger, something they can feel passionate about! Passion and a meaningful purpose is the key.

We would like to alter the way addicts see themselves, and are perceived by our community. To that end, it will be necessary for us to recognise that the negativity that follows us around, is often misplaced. With the right understanding and determination, we can be valuable members of society. We may well have distinctive and unique qualities not readily available to others, and borne of our specific genetic predispositions.

Rather than continually concentrating on the individual's "defects", trying to fathom where they are at fault, where they are damaged or defective, and perpetually pointing the finger at their weakness, we would suggest that it is our quickly moving society wherein lies the problem, addicts themselves are just born in the wrong century!

A few hundred years ago, it would have been people like me and other addicts who would have been invaluable to our tribes, teams, villages, and communities.We would have been the very ones happy to go out for days or weeks on end seeking out the fattest kill, the wildest boar because we would not have been content with the apple tree in the garden! We were "hard-wired" to need a more potent stimulus than others to feel the same reward. Needing "Bigger Better More"!

Society has moved on, but some of us still have that residual hard wiring, and the need to seek out the "biggest", the "best", the "most".This specific wiring can undoubtedly become a valuable trait if used correctly, extremely destructive if not. But either way, it should NOT be seen as a "defect".

## "Ennui"

无聊 Even before we have discovered our own "drug of choice", we have often felt a sense of "ennui", of "dissatisfaction", feeling "underwhelmed", watching while others around us got excited. We were regularly told we were "ungrateful", "greedy", "never satisfied", an accusation that was, on the face of it, undeniably true!

However, we were not necessarily selfish, but we simply did not feel the same satisfaction as others and even felt a bit cheated. Knowing how we felt, and wondering why we seemed to be so underwhelmed, it was easy for us to accept those labels "selfish", "greedy" "ungrateful", "never satisfied". And having then accepted those negative labels, and feeling ashamed, we might have spent years seeing everything about us as glaringly negative, spotlighting our "character defects", weaknesses, and" shortcomings".

Hard to think of ourselves as a valuable and irreplaceable part of the Universe when we felt lower than a snakes' belly in the grass! Our addictive drive, when left to its own devices, inevitably led us into trouble, and as our using escalated, and our behaviour deteriorated, in the grips of our addiction, and the depths it can take us, we had to concede that we were perhaps "sick" or even "bad" when in reality we were simply not wired in quite the same way.

This wiring is not, in itself, a negative trait. However, it can be unimaginably destructive. It is something that, given the right approach, can be harnessed and result in something compelling and positive.

Our hard-wired search for the "biggest, best, most" in this day and age, and the absence of the wildest boar and the fattest kill will inevitably lead us to the mind-altering chemicals which give us the biggest "buzz", the highest high. The power of that addictive brain should never be underestimated. We intend to show a new and positive slant on that which often vilified, and is one of the least understood conditions.

賦權 "Empowerment" is always our carrion cry! How, with knowledge, passion and purpose, having found a meaningful recovery, we can soar!

I am not suggesting that this will be an easy road; we would not imply it is as simple as waving a magic wand. If it were, then everyone would be waving one, and we would all live happily ever after! Would that be so!

If you are struggling in the early stages of recovery, do not kid yourself, there is hard work involved! None the less, it can be an exciting and rewarding journey, as a few of our contributors will show. Sadly, many of us have almost become comfortable with the negativity, a feeling that needs to be altered.

It would be useless just knowing a problem, without having some solutions. Experience and facts alone are not enough, so we need to look at how we can change and reverse that negativity.!
We intend to share some thoughts on how we can transform that "muck" into "manure," to nurture and cultivate a new way of looking at ourselves, and to make an exciting "Five-star restoration" outcome more possible.

## ADDICTION

*Addiction can be defined as the uncontrolled, compulsive use of a substance, person, thought, or behaviour, to change the person's emotional state, regardless of any potential consequences and against their conscious will.*

Everyone has an opinion! Put one hundred people who work in the field of substance misuse, along with a smattering of some who are in "recovery", add some of their significant "others" and ask them what addiction is all about, and what you should do about it? You will get a hundred different answers! It was ever thus.

There is nothing wrong with having opinions; of course, we all have them, including me. We have formed them over our lifetime. They are based on our background, family and social circles, education, exposure to things, and personal experiences. Add then a few genetic traits, curtesy of our ancestors!

After all, we are every one of us, a sum total of our genetic blueprint and our life events. We have formed opinions in order to survive in the world. However, when we want to understand something well, it is necessary to ditch some firmly held opinions and beliefs and look at the evidence! We think that neuroscience and epigenetics are the best way to provide this evidence.

When I first started work in this field, there were pretty much only two opinions: One was that the addiction condition was *"genetic"*, inherited from our antecedents, the other that it was *"learned behaviour"*, perhaps from our upbringing. The two factions disagreed and argued.

The problem with these two extreme views was that those who blamed "genetics" didn't always know how genes work, and those spotlighting "learned behaviour" didn't always know how learning occurs! Of course, they formed their opinions from the limited knowledge of the time. With more advanced understanding, we can look at both of those opinions, with a much more unobstructed view.

Some say addiction is "genetic" and their understanding is that this has been "passed down" by some a defected family member or ancestor- we want to unpick that idea.

Others will say that addiction is an "illness". But although there is no doubt that the addict, in the throes of his addiction is not in control, in a similar way to being "ill", nor did he choose his brain wiring, we don't see addiction as an "illness" in the accepted sense of the word. It cannot be classified as a "disease" using the usual criteria. (It is, however, undoubtedly a useful analogy in early recovery, when guilt is already so overwhelming, to see oneself as "ill".) However, if we want a real "restoration", this concept of being "ill" is limiting and disempowering.

There are plenty who will say it is a "moral weakness", or a result of "weak intellect" "poor parenting" "poverty" "trauma" "peer pressure" etc. etc. The opinions are many and varied, but almost always negative and very often judgmental. In general, all these opposing views about addicts and their plight can even be harmful. The condition is actually rooted in the interaction of the environment with genetically pre-disposed brain chemistry imbalances; addiction is a symptom of that interaction.

One's environment does not cause addiction, nor is it caused by genetic predisposition; it results from a combination of the two.

"Recovery" from addiction is not inevitable. Real recovery relies on abstinence. Unfortunately, abstinence itself is initially a powerful stressor, both physically and emotionally. The person has lost something perceived as precious: their source of pleasure, their painkiller and their emotional crutch. Relapse is very, very common.

It is all too easy for a person to think that they cannot be addicted because they have managed to stop. They will convince themselves that the chemical is not the problem, and project the problem onto other things, for example, they only used because their marriage broke down or they lost their job. The downward spiral is then resumed, control is lost, and the use of any addictor will then reinforce the conditioned learning of that behaviour. Sometimes they will swap one addiction for another, in an attempt to show their ability to "control" their using.

Our opinion is borne of years of study, scientific evidence, experience, and patient feedback that recovery requires several steps. Any therapeutic route to recovery that an addicted person chooses should, without question, fulfill all of the criteria in these steps:

1. The removal of Denial

2. Abstinence

3. In-depth learning of the truth of one's condition

4. Sustained hard work to build the ability to respond to challenge, change, disappointment.

5. The improvement of status and self-respect

6. The reductions of feelings of isolation and enhancement of connection to others.

7. The provision of emotional safety and support without collusion (tough love)

8. The reduction of stressors

9. The Empowerment of the individual

10. Finding a Passion and purpose

How can this be achieved?

1. Talking alone to the person will not be effective until the unconscious brain's craving mechanisms are supported. People spend a lot of time "talking" to the addict, but we often are "talking" to the wrong part of the brain! More of that later.

2. In our own experience, we have found that acupuncture is one of the things that can be really a beneficial contribution at this stage. (there are others) Its focus is on the modification of thought and feeling related to a neurochemical imbalance in the brain. More of that also later.

3. Denial is a creation of the addictive process. The brain shields the truth as a protective mechanism to continue to supply it with which it has fallen in love. The brain uses an unconscious process to manipulate our biochemistry. The realisation that one is powerless to the dominance of the brain helps remove denial.

4. Education regarding the reality of the craving brain empowers the individual. No longer do people assume themselves to have a moral deficit and be beyond hope. Instead, they realise that their brain is hard-wired to be truly special and of significant value when harnessed correctly.

5. Recovery starts when the person becomes aware that their condition lies in the brain's wiring. They can then learn that they are powerless to control their use of chemicals and that the substances control them. In this way, they realise that they must remain abstinent at all costs. It is sometimes easy for people to see that the problem lies in the brain, but often they see it as a "defect" which is simply not the case.

6. The support of others is of great benefit. Survival of the individual is improved with the help of family, the tribe, the pack, the group, or the team, natural selection has made it so.

7. External (systemic) stressors should be reduced as far as possible; poor education and poverty are examples of these. Schemes that offer training, jobs and housing are of incredible value.

8. Internal (process) stressors should all be tackled; a feeling of incapability to provide for the home or the family, loneliness,

depression, are examples of these. Services that offer counselling and other cognitive therapies might be sought.

9. Non-drug related behaviours must be repeatedly reinforced to condition neural pathways.

10. Family and friends should also be supported. They will also feel the stress and shame of the user. They too must not deny the problem and enable the situation to continue. The enabler must reach a point whereby they realise that they are prolonging the crisis. Organisations that provide for codependents are essential.

Interventions that aid recovery are many; addiction is much more than having problems associated with drug use. The key factors are that the person has lost control and is in denial of their situation. If the person could control their behaviour, then they are, by definition, not addicted.

They may appear to use a drug, like alcohol, in a way that seems to be alcoholic, but if they can stop and not revert to their previous habits, they were not truly addicted.

Indeed, some people who appear to be addicted can just stop using. To reiterate, they are not addicted. Unfortunately, such people's existence gives those who are genuinely addicted, a great excuse to try and continue controlling their drug use. Think about people you know. Could a heavy smoker limit their intake to just one or two cigarettes a week? Usually, they cannot, but they continue to try because they have heard of someone who can smoke occasionally, and it suits them to convince themselves that they can do this too.

Most addicts can stop, but it is the "*staying stopped*" which is necessary, and far more complicated.

It would be incredibly naive to think that one sole intervention can solve the problem of addiction; a multi-model approach is often needed . It is one thing addressing some of the underlying biological processes behind addiction, but conditioned learning and any underlying stressors must also be addressed.

There are many interventions which can be useful, equally there are very many which are not! Many services are doing a great job supporting people back to wellness. However, some services have become self-serving and rarely understand the addictive client, and in our opinion, should be avoided.

Treatment of addiction always has been the "Cinderella" of healthcare, addicts have often been a "commodity" in one form or another, argued about, and even fought over! Either to keep the large drug companies in business or the expensive treatment centres or even to keep the community charities funded.The recent trend to ask previous "service users" to volunteer to work at at these centers to keep them afloat is becoming exploitative and patronizing.

There is an expectation of low recovery. So when these inadequate responses fail, the blame is often levied at the addict himself! Or one service pointing the finger at another!
Anyone whose real agenda is the wellbeing of the person they are involved with will naturally strive for the best possible treatment for that person. I think no one will be more on the side of the addict than someone who has been there, but some wonderful people have not had an addiction and "get it" too!

We are not going to advocate a particular therapy. Still, regardless of whatever route a person chooses, we suggest that it is crucial always to ensure that the 10 points we have highlighted above are addressed.

To make a recovery possible, there is a necessity for a correct understanding of the brain, optimum brain health being crucial. The brain is the boss! It is in charge, and it is the target organ of addiction. Brain health is essential for us all, regardless of whether we have any addictions.

Real and lasting "restoration" is quite an undertaking, and seen by many as a "lifetimes journey" and as with all significant journeys, the need for adequate "fuel" is essential.

Rather than singling out a particular route, our contribution to this devastating condition is to provide some of that fuel to make those journeys more possible.

Because everyone is different, there is rarely a "one fits all" answer to any problem of this nature. We aim to support whatever particular recovery path a person may choose. There should NOT be any competition when dealing with people's lives, so our approach will enhance any programme or route to recovery.

Our genetic predispositions and life experiences mean that humans are an absolute "One-off", a unique entity. There has never been anyone like us before, and there never will be again. We are every one of us, a unique and irreplaceable part of the Universe. We are made of "Stardust"! and the same "Stardust" as everyone else, the same stardust as the Governors, Politicians, Celebrities, Presidents, the Queen, the pope!星塵

We must own our recovery, take back our power! Our "Five-star recovery" approach is designed to reconnect with some of our innate survival skills, strengthen that "stardust" quality, and to supply some of the fuel, that will be needed to empower the individual's journey to restoration

If we are to achieve a lasting "restoration" we need to be "match fit", in the same way as a prizefighter, facing a championship, would get into optimum shape. He would make sure he was eating a proper diet, getting adequate sleep, following his coach's exercise programme, he would strengthen himself for the fight and "psyche himself up"!

Our five-star approach takes the same holistic stance, and it is accessible to everyone and anyone, and can be used anywhere We all surely need to be "matchfit" because we all have our own personal battles to fight.

Our practice has been our practice to teach therapists and healthcare workers and "Empower" their clients by giving them a full understanding of the way our brains work. I feel strongly that addicts themselves should be given a chance to be in charge of their own restoration, and destiny, and only go to a professional if they have a knot they find difficult to unravel or a crisis they can't easily overcome. Those professionals should be open to scrutiny, to show their commitment to the empowerment of each individual. Sometimes there is an unhealthy power imbalance.

Regardless of the route that anyone takes, one thing we feel is entirely critical, is a connection with others; As humans, we have evolved to need each other. We learned very early on in our evolution that we were safer in tribes, packs, families.

Our ancestors learned the necessity of co-operation for their survival, and we disregard that innate knowledge at our peril. It is a human imperative to "belong". So we can see how, often because of our behaviour as active addicts, we have become isolated from that vital part of our humanity and don't function as well as we might. I for example, always felt like a perpetual "outsider", and "bad".An alien in a world that I so badly wanted to belong to and be a part of.

When we look at how other species depend on their "tribes", ants, bees, even bacteria, we must surely see how stupid we have been to think we can thrive on our own! We are a social species. Moreover, we are a benevolent species, hard to fathom when we listen to global news. But we are fundamentally benevolent; we would not have survived as a species this far if we were not.

As addicts, we have often been isolated for so many reasons, but we do need to connect with other human beings, and so it makes sense then to gather our tribe, or forge connections with new ones, strengthen those survival skills, and regain our super power! In the next chapter will talk about how we came to all of these conclusions

## Chapter Two
### The Smart-Uk story so far

It feels a bit pretentious about writing a whole book and mostly about one's own experiences and opinions !! The term "imposter syndrome" I am sure, was coined for me!

I have found it difficult to write this story without the feeling that I am conceited, an image I would hate! It was drummed into me relentlessly when I was young, to never crow about any successes! I don't seem to have a healthy "barometer" around pride in my work and humility!

But I AM proud of Smart-UK and the people I have taught, it has been a collaborative process, and I have learned as much from them as they from me! And everyone who has ever been involved should be honoured!

I always want to teach rather than lead and to make a difference in the treatment of addiction. I have now taught over twenty thousand people. So I wondered if I walked away from my work now (I am getting pretty old after all!) whether my contribution has truly made a difference?

When I first started to work in the addiction arena many years ago, it was suggested that each addict would detrimentally affect at least four more people around them. Even at the time, we always thought that this was a very conservative estimate and should perhaps have at least one zero after that figure! So by the same token, every one addict that recovers will be improving the lives of at least four more people around them, adding at the very least another zero when counting their family and friends, their community, and society as a whole.

So it is truly humbling to realise that I have personally taught 20,000 healthcare workers, who will, I know in turn, help at the very least 100 people, who will all have families and friends, colleagues, and communities, then the number seems unbelievable.

It is almost impossible to untangle the story of Smart-UK from my own story; they are so entwined! I can hardly believe how this has grown from one very un-important person (me!) who had a passion for getting things right for addicts into today's organisation. I hope it proves that anyone can make a difference.

Smart-UK came into being 24 years ago when I was practicing as a traditional acupuncturist. Along with my a private practice, I had an NHS clinic as part of our local hospital's "detox" unit, and I had already worked in that field in some capacity or other for many years. I had been in my own "recovery" at that time for over twenty years.

In the hospital clinic, I was using a five-point auricular acupuncture formula as a supportive treatment. It wasn't the only thing we did, but it certainly was a useful adjunct. The procedure was particularly "patient-friendly" they reported real benefits from improved sleep patterns to reduced cravings. They were also more inclined to stick with the rest of the treatment programme.

Later on, we found that after including this intervention within the programme, the unit had halved their medication bill! There was less demand for sleep and other extra medication, people were sleeping better, there was less itching, and generally, they engaged very much more enthusiastically in their recovery. So it was decided that it should be offered to the broader patient group and get more people trained to add it to the outpatient service, because of the demand.

There were courses around, but after some of the nurses had attended them, the hospital unit and the psychiatrist I worked alongside, weren't happy. He said he thought it all a bit "flakey". I had to agree, there were so many things that I had felt just weren't "quite right" about the existing teaching, not terrible, but just not "quite right."

They asked me if I could create some training that had a more "scientific" approach to the work, something more in line with clinical governance and for people who already knew the addiction treatment world.

When looking at what was around at the time, I was frustrated by the lack of addiction knowledge by those promoting acupuncture in its treatment—but equally frustrated by those who dismissed it! I want the best for other addicts, the "Biggest, The Best, The Most"!

I was asked to create a teaching course that fulfilled those professional needs. I felt strongly that people working with addicts should better understand the condition, and we should surely all want to keep advancing that understanding.

I also thought that anyone looking at Chinese medicine should be afforded insight into its real value. I cringed at the treatment being seen as a sort of "party trick" of minimal value, or as a "magic bullet" both of which were incorrect. I needed to honour both systems of medicine.醫學

It worried me that without a correct "translation" and application, the treatment might ultimately fall into disrepute and subsequently be lost to patients, which would have been a tragedy. My stance is not borne of arrogance, but out of a personal sense of "survivor vulnerability", based on many bad experiences!.

I had attended a course taught by an acupuncturist in London, which was around at the time. It certainly taught the ear points, but I was concerned about the lack of addiction understanding. They would say things like "addicts are all emotionally immature" which is entirely incorrect and offended me a bit!! It just wasn't "quite right". I attended another in Germany, which was similar. So because I had heard this type of treatment had been pioneered in America, I went there also to see for myself.

The treatment was said to have been pioneered in the Lincoln memorial hospital in the Bronx New York, and the psychiatrist credited with its discovery was Dr Michael Smith. I felt sure it would be amazing (I certainly wanted it to be!).

The Bronx had been a pretty desolate place at that time, mostly African American and Hispanic population and where there was a lot of poverty and social deprivation, and inevitably, massive mental health, drug and alcohol problems. I felt driven to go there, after being told how it was transforming substance misuse recovery.

I have to say it was quite an experience! I met some wonderful people, especially among the patients there. It's extraordinary how we addicts can always relate to others trying to recover, regardless of differences in our ages, cultures and countries! I have attended meetings all over the world, sometimes where I don't even speak their language, or they mine. But we still know exactly what each other is saying!

I met some other great people who had also gone there to learn, and I had an exciting time. I was less impressed by the teaching and treatments. The workers there didn't really understand why they were doing it, but could certainly talk a good talk! It was being sold as a "detox" treatment, which of course it cannot be. Livers are responsible for "Detox", not ears!.

There was also a lot of "mystical" talk, something that undoubtedly appeals to some people, but has little bearing on real recovery. There were large egos and elitism, which I find disturbing. The best things about it were the AA and NA meetings that were on the premises, and of course, they were facilitated by addicts themselves! And can be found anywhere in the world.

The treatment, however, absolutely did help. Still, I couldn't help thinking that it would have benefited far more patients and had far better results if it was better understood and appropriately applied. I feel strongly that people with this problem should be "empowered", not kept in the dark, or considered incapable of understanding theories. Any criticisms or suggestions were met with disinterest, and it seemed as if wanting research and clinical governance stole the "magic" away. In contrast, my feelings are that proper understanding and sharing of knowledge increases it!

Many people, then and now, say what a great place Lincoln was, usually people who have not worked in the greater addiction world before. Had they done so, they would know that the joy they witnessed was not entirely due to the place or the treatments. It was mostly down to the addicts themselves!

Wherever there are a whole group of people gathered together, all trying to get out of the devastating effects of addiction, there is often that euphoria! We say it is like the elation felt after being in the sea after a ship has sunk, finding a life raft, and then meeting others with the same euphoric relief, all are on that raft against all the odds. Being around or simply witnessing that sense of "survival" is infectious. I suspect that was what was experienced and seen by visitors but that they didn't attribute to the addicts themselves!

I was disappointed. It seemed the agenda was more about the place, the "mysticism" and less about the addict. However, I do honour the work they did and the contribution they made. Many people were helped, and that after all, has to be the only thing that matters. In fact, when I was there, we saw between 300 and 500 people a day for ear acupuncture! That suggested to me that something was working!

歷史 *History*

I have decided not to dwell too much on the history of auricular acupuncture here, this story, after all, is about Smart-Uk's journey. More importantly, it is also about the empowerment of addicts, not acupuncture or its route. In a lot of the telling, I think it becomes about the individuals, their egos, the politics and difference of opinions. The result is that the addict can get lost and the focus on the patient forgotten.

There are different strands of treatment organisations, rather like the different strands within evolution. Smart-Uk doesn't affiliate with any other; we have differences of opinions about the treatment's methodology and practice. I have no yearning to be part of a collective history, just to get on with the work. I don't get involved with other organisations; my excursions into that world haven't been pleasant. So while we acknowledge other contributions, it is a pointless exercise to be involved with people who have a fundamentally different agenda, and I don't have time or energy to waste. I make no excuses for that decision; perhaps it is my addict's" once bitten "wariness" or my survivor "hyper-vigilance!

Here we are concentrating on the empowerment of addicts and OUR evolution! None the less, I do think there is one record that should be clarified.

It has always been said that Michael Smith created this practice, and indeed he pioneered his angle of it, but I have learned more now about the Young Lords and Black Panther movement's involvement long before Michael Smith was involved.

Its origins can be traced back to the civil rights era, a history that has mostly remained outside of the usual narrative. In the '70s, the community-led Lincoln "Detox" as it came to be known, first looked at acupuncture for treatment among the local community with addiction. It was a very successful community gathering place, started primarily by Mutulu Shakur, a prominent member of the Republic of New Afrika.

It included acupuncture, political education and community support. I very much share the feelings of those involved then, who wanted to champion empowerment and for patients to have more agency over their recovery. They were railing against overprescribing by "white men in white coats in white hospitals", where there was very little being offered in terms of help, apart from the vast amount of Methadone being overprescribed, more or less as a 'chemical cosh".

The community were, quite rightly, up in arms about it. They considered their communities were being destroyed by "slum-lords, unscrupulous doctors, organised crime, greedy drug companies, methadone pushers, and corrupt cops". They warned of the dangers of Methadone, from "brainwave changes" to "cot deaths." So the Black Panthers and Young Lords ran the centre with the emphasis on more natural interventions, and with community involvement, and they saw it blossom.

In 1978, a task force of 200 police closed it down violently and threateningly saying it was poorly managed. It is still considered  that the authorities had used them as a "scapegoat" for the rest of the hospital's chaos and poor management. Later it was reopened, this time with Michael Smith.And it became quite a different programme.

So although I don't want to turn this into political history, I would like to pay homage to those earlier pioneers, who had been somewhat pushed out, and their pivotal role ostensibly written from the history. I share their sentiments.

## 地理 *Geography*

It is a mistake, usually, to try and replicate things that work very well in one country into another. There are certainly similarities, but quite a lot of differences. Faced with the dilemmas of including any protocol in addiction treatment, you have to navigate the dominant politics and opinions in your geographical region. There are so many differences between us, not least the fact that drug and alcohol treatment is free here in England.

There are some private expensive residential treatment centres, of course, but every town, every city has free access to help with addiction. Those services are, by and large honourable, but although they are considered "charities", they are effectively "businesses" and have to seek their funding based on their performance.

The criteria for effective "performance" is hugely suspect. It is often measured by how many times a worker has "engaged" with a client. Now that may mean a valuable one to one appointment, but it can just as easily be simply waving to the client over the road! The severity or nature of addiction is lost to the box-ticking and target attaining.

Because it is understood that there is a low recovery rate for addicts, that low recovery rate can serve to hide inadequate interventions. The various charities are continually trying to "undercut" each other and each year putting in a "tender" for what they offer and trying to outbid their rivals. I am very wary of volunteers enthusiasm being exploited too.

The influence of money will <u>always</u> change the dynamic, and since forever, addicts have been seen as a commodity, often exploited, argued about, rarely understood. So when looking at real recovery, it is critical to remove what is valuable and can be translated usefully and leave behind that which cannot.

Addiction should never be trivialised, the wellbeing of the client must always be paramount. It is not an exaggeration to say that addiction KILLS people!

## 智能英國 Smart-UK

When I got back to England, I knew if I was going to teach at all, it had to be from a very different perspective, with the wellbeing of the patient as the primary focus. I started in a small way; to begin with, it was just me! It wasn't welcomed too much by other organisations that were teaching. Still, I know from many years of addiction experience, how important it is to follow your own path, and knowing the severity of the condition, to be realistic and authentic.

If you begin with a fundamental misunderstanding of any condition, then everything you try and do to help it is "not quite right". I feared that a "That will do "attitude might prevail. With my addict's brain, I always want something "Bigger, Better, More" so I persevered!

I thought perhaps I would teach a few short courses a year, to those who wanted a fuller understanding, from my perspective. I said that I would teach whenever I was asked; I figured if people liked what I had to offer, then I would continue, if they didn't, then I would stop! I have never advertised, never promoted what I do, so the growth was organic, which I always feel is the best way, and beyond outside influences.

But I found that demand was continually growing and I needed to have some help, so I talked to my friend and colleague Kim Wager (Now Dr Kim!) he and I were like-minded, and so he agreed to join me, and we began creating our current teaching programme.

We had no idea how our courses would be received; we just wanted our teaching to be the very best and the most authentic we could make it. We began by teaching counsellors, nurses, doctors, those who work individually in the addiction field. That expanded to include mental health workers, and people who work with complex PTSD. Because our hypothesis can explain the treatment and why it works, without "hocus pocus", we have been able to see it included in mainstream medicine, and replicate it in so many different treatment areas. We have made many friends along the way, many of them still practicing, or have certainly stayed in touch.

We began traveling to deliver the teaching on sites. Lots of fantastic setups within local communities, and have been in awe at their commitment and care. We have taught in tiny rooms, big hospitals a nightclub and even a football stadium!

In "Combat Stress", we taught staff in the the organisation that looks after injured veterans of conflict, we have taught in The "Christie" cancer hospital, the biggest in Europe.

I have taught on the 15th floor of building on Madison Avenue in Manhattan, where I had to pinch myself when straight in front of me through the window as I taught was the Empire State building!

Small beginnings have equally inspired us; when someone with passion has created a significant change borne of their pain. I remember first teaching "Escape" in Blyth in the North East of England, an organisation started by a woman who had lost her teenage daughter to a methadone overdose, who was joined by another Mother and then another, at first supporting parents, and then addicts themselves. We have watched it grow to a community centre employing dozens of people.

I am also proud of the small group of beautiful women in Northern Ireland who are doggedly doing great work, despite a lot of opposition. The women working with street sex workers in Coventry, the one person working students with mental health difficulties, the prison staff who have often had to fight for the service. There have been too many wonderful and inspiring experiences to list.

We opened our "Smart-UK Institution" together in Leamington Spa, where we treated patients, taught some of our courses, and ran recovery groups. We employed more people to help. Louise Rooney, our operations manager for years, contributed in so many ways, including invaluable teaching input. Tina Richmond, who supported us also for many years. These days, I must thank Annie Webster, our current administrator, for her unwavering support and help, humour, and lovely energy!

Along with addiction and mental healthcare workers, we have taught people working in HIV and AIDS treatment, homeless shelters, those working in city centres for sex workers, and people in expensive private treatment centres.

We have taught psychiatrists, doctors, nurses, prison officers, counsellors, we have even taught nuns! We have trained acupuncturists too, and I travelled to North Carolina to teach qualified acupuncturists there. However, my personal preference is to teach people who already work in this field who aren't traditional acupuncturists.

## Smart-UK in prison

監獄 I cannot believe that I have now taught staff from 128 UK prisons! And continue to do so with pride and pleasure! Our programme is used in all of the maximum-security prisons, and the Dangerous Severe personality units within the prison system.

The first time we worked with anyone from prison was about 21 years ago, when two officers from the maximum-security prison, HMP Long Lartin, came along to one of our courses. They had been "sent" and were both very nervous, not quite sure what to expect and were more than a little wary! But they did learn, became enthusiastic, and began including this treatment in the substance misuse treatment wing within the prison.

Shortly after that, we responded to a request to deliver a prison course in the Midlands HMP Featherstone. That time there were about twenty-five officers! I had never been to a prison before and didn't know what to expect, but the experience for me was life-changing! Not only were the officers bright and easy to teach, but they also taught me as much as they learned! And I don't think I have ever laughed so much in my entire life as we were introduced to that unique prison humour!!

Here in the UK, I consider we have the best prison system in the world, and our officers and the civilian staff, are professional, humourous, humane, and honourable. Prison staff the world over get a lot of very much undeserved bad press, and I, for one, feel very privileged to work alongside them all.

All of the prisons have their own character, and I have had many precious experiences! I visited Oscar Wilde's cell in Reading prison, which had a blue plaque on the wall! I was taken around the "Mulberry Bush" in Wakefield prison. I was shown how the building, which is now the segregation unit, used to be the women and children's "workhouse". As in the old nursery rhyme, "Here we go round the Mulberry Bush on a cold and frosty morning", they were allowed to go twice around the Mulberry bush for exercise! The next verse was "This is the way we wash the clothes" which was of course what they did all day. They worked as a laundry. That bush has a preservation order on it now.

I was shown a "crank machine" that in Victorian times had been used as a hard labour punishment, and prisoners had to turn the machine's handle, which was filled with sand or water to make it harder to turn. The prison guard could tighten a screw on the drum to make it even harder, hence the slang name "screw" for prison officers!

I have seen ancient "punishment" paraphernalia, seen where they hanged the last man in England, but most of all, I have witnessed unquestionable kindness and compassion.

In Six High-security prisons, along with our friend and colleague Michael Wheatley, and Cambridge University, we conducted the first research into this protocol with remarkably positive results. We intend to embark on more research shortly, this time with a scientific stamp.

## 演化 *Evolution*

As we grew, researched and studied, our greater understanding of the addictive brain emerged. As human beings, we learn everything this way, adding to what we already know. Humans have built up our survival tools over lessons learned throughout our lifetime, similarly to the way we build, our immune systems.

We know that everything that happens to us makes us who we are. Everything we have learned will inform what we think and know now. There's no doubt we have discarded a lot of the things we learned as children, but the results of that learning do remain. We may have forgotten the details, but their impact on us is still part of who we are.

So although this book seems to have several tangents, they have all been instrumental in its evolution. I often wish I could teach all the people that we taught in the first 20 years again! We have learned so much more.! If I had my life back, and it could have been "normal" I would have loved to work in some capacity in science or anthropology, it holds a great fascination for me. It is not always the case that our lives, and our careers, take a straight forward linear route, often we have taken a very "curved path", we may have been to many places before we get to "here". And in doing so have learned things along the way. I have very much loved my Chinese medicine practice!

Survivors of abuse, like me, notably tend to have a very checkered path, our education often interrupted, our employment record sketchy. Our route was tortuous and twisted. During my growing up and my "recovery," and as a single parent of six children, I had to do many jobs! I have worked in hundreds of bars and clubs, hospitals, shops, offices, restaurants, a factory, even a mill! I ran my own restaurant, and I was once a magician's assistant, getting my head "chopped off" and being sawn in half! I started nursing, which was not really for me, but mostly did whatever I could get paid for, until ultimately, after getting into recovery, I went back to "school"!

無權無勢的人们 I have always felt most comfortable with other dis-enfranchised people, so I guess it was inevitable that I became a counsellor in the field of substance misuse, a subject very close to my heart. I did that for many years.

In latter years, often I have found I am asked to justify, especially to some skeptical acquaintances, that what I do in my "day job" is practice Chinese Medicine! I have been a practicing acupuncturist for 25 years.

I have found throughout these years there is much pretension on both sides! Some scientists can be very arrogant and dismissive, and some Chinese medicine practitioners seem to think they have a monopoly on caring! I think both attitudes are unfortunate.

Naturally, I appreciate the skepticism surrounding anything that people don't understand; indeed, I am the biggest skeptic! But no matter how indifferent you are, you cannot casually dismiss, without proper investigation, a whole system of medicine which has been used effectively in the East and elsewhere for millennia!

There is an unfortunate tendency to lump acupuncture in with things like "homeopathy" and "crystal healing". When, of course, Chinese medicine is nothing at all like them.

The difficulty has been that although there is little doubt about the efficacy of this practice, there is plenty of research to that effect, the usual explanations of it in the West, are inadequate and outmoded. There is a great reluctance on the part of many to let go of ancient terminology which has no place in modern clinical practice.

The problem I think lies with the singers rather than the song! We consider that although acupuncture dates back thousands of years, it must keep pace with the modern world. It is our opinion that acupuncture is, or at least should be, approached like any other science and if it is to be accepted in the West, be treated as such. From the standpoint of science, if there is no proof for any theory's validity, it remains just that, theory. Until a theory is substantiated, it cannot yet be accepted as fact.

There is no mysticism, If we are working with the human body, then we must, by definition, be working with biology, and therefore by reduction chemistry, and by further reduction physics!

Our approach, by no means, invalidates Chinese medical practice. What is of significant concern to us are the ingenious explanations given in the West, for Chinese practice, some of which we consider to be no longer valid in the face of current scientific knowledge.

古代文化 Chinese culture is ancient and very different from that in the West. It is a whole way of living and view of the Universe handed down from ancestors that is very much weaved into people's daily lives. I don't think that essence can be captured by merely using terminology that is not common parlance in the West. But it is quite possible to translate those terms into language that we all understand and to which we can relate. It is also possible for we westerners to view the Universe through that Chinese lens.

 While the terminology of the past is endearing, it is that reluctance of many practitioners to challenge old models that hinder the acceptance of acupuncture into the mainstream. That is not to say treatment practices are outdated, but that the previously described mode of action is incorrect. There is a tendency to use that terminology to create a kind of mystical elitism. For example, we realised that the point names used for the auricular treatment had no clinical reality, and we felt they caused fear or false hope with patients. Hence we changed them to numbers to reflect the formula itself, and which were less emotive.concentrating more on the overall outcomes rather than the specific point names.

 Rather than perpetuate any mystical narrative, We demonstrate that auricular acupuncture points stimulate branches of cranial nerves, mainly the somatic trigeminal nerve, and the autonomic vagus nerve.

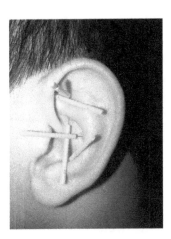

These go on to innervate specific brain regions, such as the raphe nuclei of the reticular formation, and the somatosensory cortex.

I promised to keep the brain stuff simple! So suffice to say, these theories have been borne out by current neuroscience research. We much prefer evidence-based practice.

## Chapter Three
### Studying

I first began studying Chinese medicine after my son Nick's death in a car crash and having had a brief period running our family vegetarian restaurant. I was looking for something meaningful to do, and addiction counseling was not bearable for me after my son's death. I needed to heal myself too from many wounds.

After Nick died, I was not fit for anything much, and I was almost suicidal again. I had been treated by a local acupuncture practitioner, Sarida Browne, who had helped me enormously. I felt I was on a healing path. Then while serving in our restaurant, I met people studying at the local acupuncture college and had become fascinated by the poetic nature of its theories.

I was asked to be a "class patient" for one of the student's exams, and then I became even more fascinated by it. I decided to try and learn it! I wasn't sure I would even get a place to study at that college; the impression they gave was that it was VERY selective!

It was there that I met my colleague and friend Dr Kim Wager, he was just eighteen, and a science student. Medicine fascinated him; his father had been an ionic physicist and had imbued him with the love of all things scientific. Kim had been on the point of beginning medical school when he was taken to the far East and witnessed a different kind of approach. Fascinated, he decided to come back and study it.

When Kim and I met, it was the first day at Acupuncture college. I was so delighted to have got that place, I had worked hard to meet the criteria, and as I had been away from science learning for many years, I put my name down to do an extra "science" day to prepare myself. Kim, fresh from A levels (A's stars in all sciences!) decided on that extra day, having been told he perhaps should "get up to speed". (It was, of course, more money for the extra day!) We found ourselves sitting together. I was grateful for him because I was nervous. We both had wanted to begin in the best way possible.

The day was quite ridiculous. We realised more or less immediately that this had been a waste of our time, not to mention money. It consisted of some elderly retired - psychiatric nurse passing around Grey's anatomy and showing us pictures! They knew even less than I did, and probably had only a fraction of Kim's knowledge. It wasn't even GCSE standard.

We were both on the verge of quitting several times during the first years, but neither of us is a quitter, and besides, we had paid a lot of money for the course, so we persevered, and despite the thirty years difference in our age, we became best friends along the way.

We began to see inadequacies in that college, many gaping holes in the teaching, so we went on to further courses and did a lot of our own research and study.

At that time, pretty much everyone else in that field hung on every word of a particular "Professor", marketed as some kind of Guru. It was great marketing! He was talked about as if he was a kind of magical being! As we know, perception often becomes a reality, and many people in this field seem to swallow this sort of hubris and be in need of a guru.

With my abuse survivor "hyper-vigilance" and Kim's searching scientific mind, it wasn't too long before we discovered that he wasn't a "professor" in the accepted sense of the word. He had simply been out to China at some point, as a sort of "work experience", and because the Chinese had been impressed that a Westerner wanted to practice their medicine, they "gave" him the title. He was puffed up and wore it like a crown!

It is common in China for anyone who teaches anything to be referred to as "Professor", as a sign of respect. When I think how hard Kim and other friends have had to work for their doctorates, and for how many years, it is offensive to both them and the Chinese culture to think of that kind of misuse and arrogance. 智慧

It was an expensive course, and we soon gathered that we had not been particularly "special" in getting our places after all - we simply had to be able to pay! I was often disillusioned and disappointed, but it DID begin my study into Chinese theory, and despite the "singers" I did learn a lot from the "song" I found it quite beautiful and it resonated deeply with me. So I am thankful for that initiation!

After I qualified, I even practiced at the college clinic for a while, but it was not the place for me! I went out on my own. As we learned, something quite magical did begin to happen, and that was the way Kim and I evolved as a duo! As Kim learned about acupuncture and later Chinese Herbal medicine, as a scientist, he wanted to know more and more about the neurobiology behind it all, and he returned to studying neuroscience. In doing so, he also ignited my passion for science. I dragged him into my world of addiction treatment, and we both wanted to explain the neurobiology of that!

We began to formulate our hypotheses with my passion and experience, and Kim's knowledge and, despite some opposition to our stance, we took the baton and ran with it in our teaching work. We created a teaching organisation for substance misuse "SMART-UK" which has gained a reputation for ethical good practice and integrity.智能英國
We travelled thousands of miles all over the country and abroad together, in fact, we saw more of each other than we did of our respective families, and we talked and talked incessantly! We still do!

Over the years we have had several people wanting to be involved, and whenever we have allowed it, it has been disastrous! Too many other "agendas" or attempts to exploit our work has muddied that particular water. One man's ambition nearly destroyed us. We realised that we had to keep it very much between the two of us and stay true to our vision.

We offered our scientific hypothesis in our book "Auricular Acupuncture and Addiction - mechanisms, methodology and practice". We did the first proper research into the treatment. That research, although now somewhat outdated, can be found in that book.

As we grew, we identified needs for the people we taught and their clients, so we developed a range of products that they can access without going elsewhere and paying the earth.

Kim has gone on to more considerable research as a doctor of neuroscience. However, we talk regularly, and he still has a significant influence on my work. Kim keeps abreast with all current neuroscience thinking and research, which he passes on to me! We are delighted by the recent research into Vagal nerve stimulation which validates a lot of our theories.

Most recently, I have been privileged to be able to expand my teaching to include prisoners. I created a Smart-UK "5 Star wellbeing" programme which is exciting and innovative. It came about after I was asked by one prison if it were possible to teach prisoners acupuncture to use on each other. Professionally, I didn't think that would be a good idea, for so many reasons, not least insurance.

However, there is no reason that they couldn't learn the theories, in more depth than they usually are told. I teach them about the brain, the Chinese theories, why they should access the treatment within the prison, and give them other "empowerment" tools like acupressure, nutrition, meditation etc. to help support recovery and wellbeing, for themselves and their peers. They learn everything other than the clinical procedure of putting in needles.

Initially, I was asked to go and provide a couple of days of theory, but the men engaged with it so thoroughly and got so involved that between us we created a training programme for some of them to become "Five-star wellbeing coaches". This project has become one of my absolute passions, and I am so proud of the staff and men of HMP Holme House who helped me make it possible. More from them later!

So although this book is NOT about acupuncture, it has certainly been a big part of its evolution! In Chinese theory, there are some real jewels of knowledge that have been, and are, still incredibly helpful to me and that I have been able to pass on to others. I love how I can use the simple "Five-Element" and "Yin Yang" theories as metaphors to explain complicated patterns and take the mysticism and obscure terminology out of it.

*The Smart UK course now.*

*Chinese theories.* These philosophies are not exclusive to medicine or practitioners; they are what underpins much of Chinese thought. They are a simple way of describing, by analogy, cycles of change that occur naturally, actually an excellent way of looking at everything in the Universe, including human beings.

智慧The ancient Chinese had always looked very carefully at nature, at the daily and seasonal cycles, and they recognised that, as humans, we are very much part of the natural world, as much as the trees the animals, the planets etc. All equally subject to natural laws, (The laws of physics!).

Because we are a sophisticated species, and can now build houses, and don't have to go "hunter-gathering." any more, we naively think that we are apart from nature, but that is entirely untrue.

The ancients observed that everything in the Universe was cyclical. We only have to think about herd migration, bird migration, opening and closing of plants, birth, SAD, menstruation, day and night etc. to recognise those cycles.

In the West, a lot of what we first learned regarding human bodies has been through post-mortem. The ancient Chinese didn't dissect bodies. It was not in their culture, so pretty much everything they learned was simply by very close observation of people in health and out of health. That observation was all they had, so they did it very well. They passed on to us useful and straightforward models of understanding that today, actually pretty much anyone can use.

They noted the observable changes that occurred when someone went from wellness to illness, and these became honed skills after observation of thousands of people over hundreds of years. Distinct and recurring patterns became apparent, and they became adept at spotting patterns of imbalance in humans, often long before symptoms become severe.

They became experts at seeing the changes in colour, sound, odour, and emotion of human beings, and the imbalances of their lifestyles, and that is why they were so successful at treating them. 智慧 This practice is NOT magic, nor do practitioners have the monopoly on these philosophies; they are a way of understanding the Universe and the survival skills that all human beings have, They are a bit like body language - innate skills, developed by our ancestors for survival and passed onto us. We humans didn't even have to learn them!

The study of them simply enables further understanding of the human condition, to hone our skills to help others, treat them, and measure their progress. Human beings are, undoubtedly the most magnificent of species!

These days I get much pleasure from science, despite being too old to do much more than vicariously learn from Kim!. And I have been privileged to meet many other incredible scientists and philosophers who continue to inspire me.

I no longer feel the need to justify my acupuncture studies because they were the route I took to get to where I am now! I hope I have been able to absorb the best of all study and disregard the worst. 智慧 I have learned some great gems of wisdom while studying Chinese medicine, which has informed my teaching in the same way that physics has done, I try and honour both systems. I am certainly not the "Hocus Pocus" variety of Acupuncturist, I respect, and am too excited by science for that.

None the less I have loved my acupuncture practice, my patients and my students. I love the poetic nature of the Chinese theories; Those wonderfully simple analogies can help us understand many of the world's complicated systems. So when we begin learning all about the brain, which is THE most complex complicated thing in the entire Universe, it makes perfect sense to me to embrace and utilise them.

## Chapter Four

### YIN YANG

---

腦子 The Brain

In this chapter, I want to look at the human brain, that most complicated and powerful organ, that we all have sitting on our shoulders and that we often take for granted! In our first book, Kim describes it in much more academic detail, here I want to simplify it so that all of us might wonder in its power and begin to look after it with more exceptional care. Optimum brain health is essential for everyone!

It is said that our brains are still pretty much the same as they were in cavemen's days. There is some truth in that, biologically, the human brain that has invented all our modern technology, is the same that hunted sabre tooth tigers in pre-history! And many of our instincts, and emotions, which our ancestors' needed to survive, influence much of our behaviour today, sometimes in detrimental ways! I think there have been some evolutionary changes, but we still are basically cavemen!

When we are talking about addiction, it is essential to examine the brain and the way it works. The brain is the target organ of addiction.

But first, to do that, I shall put on my "Chinese medicine" head, and introduce the famous theory of Yin/Yang, it will make looking at the brain a whole lot easier!

## YIN/YANG

The very familiar image
symbolises the Yin Yang theory.

This is often seen as a"hippy" symbol, (who hasn't had a pair of earrings or a tattoo of this at some point in our lives!) But obviously, it is far more than a hippy symbol, it is an valuable theory which underpins all Chinese thought.

It is simply put, the symbol for *"balance"*. 平衡 In all medicine, as in life, balance is critical. This theory is the Chinese way of looking at that balance. Not just for medicine, we can look at anything in the Universe in terms of Yin/ Yang.

The origins of Yin-Yang stem from ancients observation of the day and night cycle. The first reference to it was recorded in about 700 BCE. These observations are borne out by the recent scientific study of circadian rhythms,(chronobiology)

They noticed that as humans, we beat very definitely to the rhythm of the planet too. We exist as a result of natural laws, and nature is very much linked to time. Consider, for example, menstruation, birth, SAD, herd migration, bird migration, opening and closing of plants. They are all cyclical and linked to time. As humans, we too have our own internal "body clock".

Chinese writing is consisted of "pictograms" of the words to be described.

These are symbols for Yin and Yang

Yin                                      Yang

You will notice the arrows that are pointing to part of the symbols which are common to both; this is the symbol for "mountain"
On "Yin" symbol you will see a line for the horizon, underneath which is shade, so we can look at this as representing "The shady mountain" or the shady side of a mountain, or a mountain at night. On the "Yang" symbol, we see a "mountain" again, this time the sun is above the horizon line, and rays of light below it, so we can look at theYang symbol as "A sunny mountain" or the sunny side of a mountain, or a mountain in the daytime.

**YANG**
**Sunny**
**mountain**

**Yin Dark**
**mountain**

The Yin and Yang mountain images are useful when we want to look at how the Yin/Yang theory can be utilised.

Imagine sitting on that Yang sunny mountain or in the daytime. How will you experience the world around you? Think of things like temperature, moisture levels, activity?

On that Yang mountain, you would expect to feel warm, it would be dry, and if you look around there might be birds, bees, insects, so there will be activity on that mountain.

By comparison, if you were to sit on that Yin mountain, you would expect to feel cold, it would be damp, and if you look around there will be little or no activity.

So Yin things are:

- Dark
- Inactive
- Calming
- Cold
- Wet
- Contracting

The analogy we often use for YIN is WATER 水

By contrast, Yang things are:

- Light
- Active
- Stimulating
- Hot
- Dry
- Expanding

The analogy we often use for YANG is FIRE

The body needs balance, and we need to stay alive and well. Of course, we are quite able to cope with change for a while, and we don't need to be wrapped in cotton wool, but not for too long, for example, if you were to sit in a sauna for 20 minutes, you would be perfectly fine, maybe a bit hot and sweaty but not ill. If however, you were to sit in it for a whole day, you would be good and sick! It would be far too long to be in there. Equally, you wouldn't sit in a furnace for even a second; it is far too severe!

Our ability to get well or survive will be dependent on the severity of what we are exposed to, or the length of time we are exposed to it. How we bounce back, or indeed if we bounce back, will be determined by those two factors.

So with that information in mind, let us go back to our "mountains" again.

Imagine yourself sitting on that "Yang" sunny mountain again, only this time there has been a landslide, and you can't get into the shade, can't get a refreshing drink, How do you think your body will complain about this?

We may be sweating, that is our body's way of cooling us down. We may be thirsty and have a dry mouth, evident signs of dehydration, we may have a rapid pulse, shallow breathing, feel hot. We may have dark, scanty urine, (not much water around), and maybe constipation, for the same reason. We may also have insomnia and agitation.

Because by and large "Yang conditions" are "hot" nature.
Fever
Sweating
Sore throat
Thirsty, dry mouth
Scanty dark urine
Constipation
Insomnia restlessness

Now let look at the other way around, this time    you are sitting on that "Yin" cold mountain, but this time there has been an avalanche, and you can't get a hot drink, you don't have a woolly jumper, there no firewood. How is your body going to tell you this time that there is something wrong?

We won't be sweating this time, and so the body doesn't need to cool us down.

We may have slowed heartbeat and slow breathing. We may feel cold, have goosebumps and shiver. We might have pale profuse urine, more water around this time, we may have diarrhoea, for the same reason. We might also feel lethargic and have no energy.

Because by and large, Yin conditions are "cold" in nature

Chills
No sweating
Runny nose
No thirst
Profuse pale urine
Diarrhea
lethargy

 So you can perhaps see how this analogy might be useful in my clinic? The treatment principal is to use opposite treatments to bring about balance .
        For example, I might ask a patient what time of day they feel at their best or worst? If it is a physical condition, I might ask "Is it better with movement or keeping still?"
        I might have two people with arthritic knees. When I examine one patient's knee, it is cold and stiff (YIN). The other patient's knee might be hot and swollen (YANG). They both have "arthritis", but I would treat them differently because they are manifesting differently.
        It is common to see wet "oozing" eczema or dry, scaly eczema. Both conditions are labelled "eczema", but I will treat them differently because they are manifesting differently.
        A YANG headache feels as if the top of your head is blowing off! Pounding, like a hangover headache or a headache from High blood pressure.
        By comparison, a YIN headache will feel more like a tight band being squeezed around the head.
They are both labelled "headache", but I will treat them differently because they are manifesting differently.
Remember, these theories are not just about medicine; You can look at anything in the Universe in terms of Yin and Yang.

"HYPER" things are Yang

Hyper-activity

Hyperthermia

Hyper stimulation

HYPO things are YIN

Hypo-activity

Hypothermia

Hypo stimulation

Even branches of the autonomic nervous system

Sympathetic nervous system

Para-sympathetic nervous system

So you have the accelerator pedal!

and the break pedal!

We chose a couple of hormones also to demonstrate

Adrenaline,Thyroxin

(Speeding up hormones)

Corticosterone, Oestrogen

(Cooling down Hormones)

When exploring the brain and addiction, another useful way to use the Yin/ Yang analogy is to compare YIN to "fuel." It provides the material basis, the pure *POTENTIAL.* 潜在

Yang makes things happen, and it is the energy that transforms. Without YANG action, YIN would do nothing and remain merely POTENTIAL. For example, YIN fuel needs the YANG spark pugs to interact to make the engine spring to life.

Yin Fuel
Plus

Yang Spark plugs

*Engine springs to life!*

We know there is a lot of potential energy in the fuel, but on its own, it remains pure potential, nothing else.

Think of a candle, unlit, just the wax and the wick.
We are aware that there is a lot of "potential" energy in
a candle, but if it is to be useful, we have to do
something to it; otherwise, the candle will just sit on
your shelf doing nothing but gather dust.

If we light a match to the candle YANG, it is transformed, and the
candle provides heat and light

So YIN and YANG need to interact for things to happen.

The YIN/YANG theory, like all theories, must have rules
applied to make the theory work.

The first rule is "Opposition.": Not difficult to see that they are
opposite, dark, light, etc.

YIN and YANG aren't substances in themselves; they are descriptive
terms, in the same way, that "Hot" or "Cold" aren't "things" in
themselves, they are merely words to describe something.

YIN and YANG are descriptions of relativity. So they depend entirely
on the viewpoint of the observer.

So if we compare water to steam, water would be
considered relatively more YIN.

If, however, we compared Water to ice, water would be considered
relatively more YANG.

Water didn't change, just the relative viewpoint.

**YANG**    Steam
Water    **YIN**
Ice

*"Mutual consumption"*: is the next rule.
That sounds a bit unpleasant! But what it simply means is that "An excess of one, will induce a decrease in the other"
It seems common sense to see that if we have too much "Fire", it will dry up the "Water". And too much "Water" will put out the "Fire"!
What we are aiming for always is "Balance"! 平衡

So using this analogy, we can now look at the "energetics" of drugs and alcohol. Let's begin by examining the effects of "cravings".Not just withdrawal symptoms, because they are only part of the picture.
Firstly think about *"Stimulants"*, so things like Crack, Speed, Cocaine, Nicotine. When we look at how people manifest when they are craving these chemicals, we will see symptoms like "feeling hot", sweating, thirst and dry mouth. They might be sleepy but have insomnia, be anxious, agitated, angry, maybe paranoid, maybe even psychotic. Not hard to determine that these chemicals are YANG in nature.
Now let's look at the other end of the pharmaceutical spectrum, *"Depressants"*, so things like Alcohol, Heroin, Tranx, Benzodiazepines.

You would think because they are the opposite ends of the pharmaceutical spectrum. that the cravings for these chemicals would naturally be YIN in nature. BUT When we see how people manifest when they are craving them; they might be hot, sweating, sluggish, but unable to sleep, agitated, anxious, angry, shaky, maybe paranoid etc. What will strike us as strange about these two lists is that they are VERY similar! Both are YANG, not what we want to expect!

To clarify this anomaly, it is useful to think of the human body as a cauldron, full of liquid (YIN). Underneath the pot is a fire (YANG).
Above it, there are bubbles and steam.
If I were to take some cocaine, for example, you would expect to see more steam and bubbles, because a chemical like Cocaine will stoke up the fire, adding fuel and

make things hotter. (YANG) If I were then to take some Heroin or alcohol, you would see those bubbles and steam reduce, or even disappear.

You would be forgiven for thinking that you are "balancing" things out, adding more fluid, turning the heat down. (YIN) But that can't be so, because when you come off those chemicals and begin to crave them, the symptoms will be hot (YANG). What is happening is that those chemicals are masking the hot symptoms, putting a lid on the cauldron. You have then created a "pressure cooker"!
All the substances of misuse create more heat.: Stimulants stoke up the fire beneath the pot (our body) whereas Depressants put a lid on it.

That is why, although withdrawal symptoms may differ. from chemical to chemical, cravings will be the same, and all are YANG! When talking about this Yin -Yang balance, I am reminded of those old fashioned cars that needed a "crank handle" to wind them up! Think about all those black and white movies. They were nearly all about cars breaking down! In those scenarios, the driver would get out, scratch his head, and kick the car!

He soon found that they don't work any better by being kicked! So he cranked the handle, and the vehicle might splutter and stop. He would then swear and push, to no avail. Then perhaps his passenger would get out, HE would kick and swear at
the car, then they would both push, the car might go for a few inches and then stop!

At no stage do either one of them think "It might be a good idea to put some fuel in"! And we do that all the time! We might even put it on peoples assessment forms "Lack of motivation" we say, when perhaps "Lack of fuel" might be    a fairer observation!

If we look at the "cycle of change" diagram that is often used, we see that the directive is to try to get someone from pre all contemplation, into contemplation, and then into action. But that is all about movement! How can we possibly "move" without enough fuel! There is no capacity for the kind of movement needed

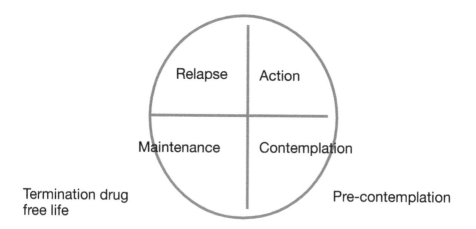

Relapse | Action

Maintenance | Contemplation

Termination drug free life

Pre-contemplation

We expect people to go the extra mile and more to recover, but how on earth can they do that when they simply do not have the fuel! They are entirely "running on empty! Then we misdiagnose their lack of full for **"Lack of motivation"!!**
So our task is to fill that up that fuel! The first step to **Empowerment** is to restore that **POTENTIAL!**

潜在

So now, with our Chinese YIN Yang theory under our belt, in the next chapter we will examine the brain

## Chapter Five
### TheBrain

The first thing we see when we look at the human brain, immediately is how very well it is protected! The brain is surrounded by the hard skull, that bony structure that protects it. It is, in fact, the most protected part of our body, which should tell us how vital it is to us!

It comes in two "halves", (hemispheres) and weighing about 2 lbs it is the consistency of Tofu: Not as tough as meat, but tougher than jelly. The two halves are physically identical, although it is generally considered that one half is more emotional and the other more linear.

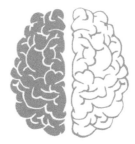

The building blocks for the human body are cells. The brain is made up of incredibly busy cells -Neurons. Unlike other cells which seem relatively simple, neurons look quite complicated.

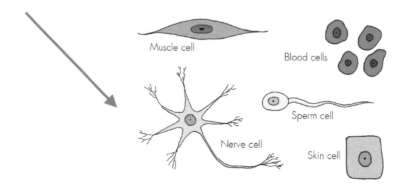

Often in nature, we can see what job something does by its shape, we only have to think about our ear which is "shell-like" our nose who's shaping conjures up the idea of smelling things, etc. etc. The neuron is no different, so when we look at it, we can almost see what its job might be, because neurons are chatty bits of equipment, they like to talk to each other! Around the cell body (the soma)you will see that there are branch-like looking things called dendrites. "Dendrite" is the Greek word for branches. They are the metaphorical

Neuron

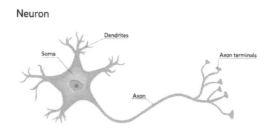

"ear-piece" of the neuron, listening out for messages from a previous neuron. That message is then passed down a wire "axon" to the metaphorical "mouthpiece of the neuron, the "terminal boutons." We have individual neurons, they are in pathways, and those pathways are in regions of the brain. All the regions are responsible for different functions, but they all do what they do because of neurons talking to each other!

So we can almost think of our brains as enormous circuit boards. We have this dense forest like collection of neurons and connections, all chatting incessantly, giving instructions to every single function that we have. We have this incredible "neural chatter" going on all the time, never stopping.

Now, when we look back at that neuron, you will see that the wire (axon) is more like a string of sausages than a cable. There are gaps along it. That gap is called a "Synapse", and those synapses are incredibly talented!

The messages are electrical. When a message comes from the previous neuron in the pathway, it passes down the axon towards the terminal boutons, ready to be passed on to the next neuron. However, with the gaps along that axon, the electrical information cannot pass.

That is where the next things to consider come into the picture: Neurotransmitters. These are chemical messengers; there's a clue in the name, they transmit messages across the synapse to the other side, a bit like a ferry.They are all different shapes,

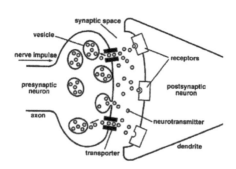

Look at the diagram of the synapse, and you can see how this works.

As the message comes along the axon, it is confronted with a gap. At one side of that gap, there are little bags called vesicles. In those vesicles are neurotransmitters, chemical messengers.

When the electrical message gets to the vesicles, the cell membrane fuses, sending the neurotransmitters out across the gap to the other side. There are "receptor sites" waiting to receive the neurotransmitters, and turn them back into electrical signals and on to the next gap!

Then when they have done their job, they go back into the gap, are broken down by enzymes, or they are taken up by a re-uptake pump which puts them back into the vesicles to use again! All very conservation-friendly!

It is a "Key and Lock" analogy., the receptor sites are different shapes, like a lock and so the neurotransmitter is like the key, it finds a shape that it fits, and opens the lock! They all individually do different things, but they all work here in this synaptic cleft. It is all to do with shape!

This neurotransmitter "key-lock analogy" is how everything we do works; the synapse is the most important thing we have. It is instructing our behaviour, breathing, muscles expanding and relaxing, everything. Everything we think, feel, imagine, or remember takes place in this gap!

All of the substances of misuse work here too.

Let's look first at things like Heroin, for example. Heroin is an "agonist", and it mimics a natural biological response in the same way as would copy the "key" and turn the "lock".

Then there are substances used as a heroin substitute like Naloxone, which is an "antagonist" and what that does is similar to "super-glueing" the lock. So that after that, when Heroin is introduced, it won't work. Antagonists are sometimes used to save someone from a heroin overdose. It can do this because the receptor site has a preference for an antagonist, and so it will kick the Heroin out in favour of the antagonist, and the person survives, if it is administered in time.

Naloxone

Substances like Subutex, are "Partial agonists" These chemicals do have a biological response, but not a complete one, a bit like fitting the key in the lock and turning it, opening the door with the chain on.

Subutex

If we think about other chemicals, things like Seroxat, Prozac, we call these SSRI's "Selective Serotonin Re-uptake Inhibitors."

Seroxat                                    Prozac

What they do is "sit" in the re-uptake pumps and they "select" a specific neurotransmitter- Serotonin. When serotonin has done its job, it falls back into the synapse. If enzymes do not break it down, it should be able to return to the vesicles via the re-uptake pump. However, if the SSRI's are blocking them, the neurotransmitter stays in the synapse longer and continues to affect the receptor site.

Cocaine does a similar thing, it "sits" in the re-uptake pump, and when it's favoured neurotransmitter Dopamine has done it it's thing, it can't get back into the vesicles and so stays around longer, and has a greater effect.

*All substance work like this*, they may block up pumps, mimic natural rewards, etc. but they all work here.

Even poisons work like this: If you have read old fashioned murder/mystery novels, you may have come across a poison called "Bella Donna." Much favored to bump people off with! It seems perverse to call a poison after the Italian for "beautiful lady", but there is a reason for the name.

What Bella Donna does if we ingest it is stop the neurotransmitter that allows muscles to contract. So we can breathe in, as the muscle which is our diaphragm expands, but can't breathe out because the diaphragm is unable to contract.. We can breathe in, but not out!

Bella Donna gets its name from the time when we first realised that enlarged black pupils were attractive, or showed that we were aroused.

So we used black eyeliner and loads of mascara to make our eyes look bigger and with darker pupils!
In the nineteenth century, when the ladies of the day were getting ready to go off to the "tea dances" in the hope of picking up Mr Darcy or the like, they would drip Bella Donna into their eyes!! It had the effect of expanding the iris, so making the pupils large and black, and so off they went feeling very attractive! Bit of a downside: they weren't able to see very well! So they may very well have gone home with someone other than Mr Darcy! This we feel was the forerunner of the "Beer Goggles"!
You may also have heard of this pretty little "Fugu" fish, or Pufferfish as he is often called. He's an innocuous-looking little thing- but he is deadly poisonous!!
His brain and spinal cord are awash with a particularly deadly poison called "Tetrodotoxin" which will kill you pretty quickly!

Tetrodotoxin

We think of poisons as attacking our "system", and
indeed they do, but in reality, they have to begin their
journey, right here in the synapse.

There are about 86billion neurons, and 100
neurotransmitters that fall into four categories,
> Excitatory Neurotransmitters
> Inhibitory Neurotransmitters
> Modulatory Neurotransmitters
> and Neuro-hormones.
> Kim discusses them in depth in our other book. But here we are
concentrating on two that are of particular concern when we talk about
addiction and other mental health conditions.:
Dopamine and Serotonin. The ones associated with pleasure and
satisfaction.

Dopamine                                    Serotonin

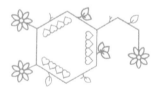          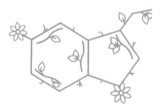

Dopamine is the primary neurotransmitter of the reward
pathway. It is responsible for anticipation, excitement, fear, anger,
paranoia , anxiety insomnia, motivation, and activating the adrenaline
system. If something feels good it is because Dopamine is present. We
think of Dopamine as YANG in nature.
Serotonin is then needed to provide a "full stop" because it is
associated with: Sleep, satiation, calming, relaxing, and it also
modulates the Dopamine system. We think of Serotonin as YIN in
nature.

To demonstrate how important this is, we often imagine some "Neurotransmitter cookery"!

Thinking of Dopamine as red hot chili pepper! We consider what would happen if we rubbed red hot chill pepper into our eyes? it would be damned painful, and quite a bit stupid of course, but we are more concerned with what the eyes would do about it? Well, they would water of course, produce some YIN to counteract the YANG for balance.

Now imagine we were really really stupid, and kept on rubbing the chillie pepper into our eyes? The eyes would try and cope, producing tears to cool the eyes down.But over time they would dry up! the YANG pepper is too severe and we are repeating the rubbing too!

Remember our ability to recover from anything will depend on the severity of the problem, or how long we have been exposed to it! The brain does this too!

Dopamine is the primary neurotransmitter of the reward pathway.All the substances of misuse increase Dopamine in the reward pathway.Although they act through separate mechanisms.

Drugs that are not abused don't affect concentrations of Dopamine in the reward pathway.So for example we don't get addicted to antibiotics or the contraceptive pill.

Serotonin is needed to provide satisfaction. Over time it can't cope and it "dries up". It is more fragile that Dopamine, and more complicated, so if it gets depleted, it takes longer to produce more. Remember that law of "Mutual consumption"?

An excess of one will cause a decrease in the other!

The extremely YANG chemicals, increasing Dopamine plus the equally YANG chaotic behaviour causes a depletion of the YIN Serotonin! We have now run out of fuel!

The "fuel we have been talking about is actually Serotonin.

This is important to understand, because while ever we are concentrating on the chasing of Dopamine, we are disregarding the more important fact that it is an inability of Serotonin to modulate that Dopamine system.

## Pleasure 樂趣

So now let's consider what kind of activities give pleasure to most human beings? And why pleasure is essential?
In our teaching courses, and when we get a "brainstormed" list of pleasures together - we always see the same ones!!

*Sex- Food-Friends and Family-Exercise and Sport-Music and Dancing-Animals - Sunshine- Senses -Shopping- Films and Books.*
Many other things give humans pleasure, and there will always be individual variances, but those are the usual ones that come to mind. So Why? Why is pleasure so important? It certainly does make us feel good, and it balances out the bad stuff, but nature doesn't work like that, there has to be a good biological reason for it!
The answer, of course, lies in our need for our  SURVIVAL!

<u>Sex</u> is obviously about survival! If we didn't have sex, we wouldn't reproduce, and the species might die out! That doesn't feel very romantic, but there it is! Sex is probably the most significant "pleasure hit" that most humans can have. Mother Nature makes sex pleasurable so we will do it again!

<u>Food</u> is definitely about survival! If we didn't eat, we wouldn't survive. Interestingly, the foods that give the greatest pleasure, that taste the best seem to be the ones with the highest calorific content- the sugary foods, fatty foods etc. All the ones that we have to give up if we are on a diet! We rarely have to give up celery sticks!
This all stems from a time when food was scarce, and we had to find food with most calories in case we couldn't find any more! Nature wants us to survive, so attaches pleasure to foods that will help. we no longer need to pile up the calories, food is usually plentiful, but we still have that ancient wiring sadly, that prefers fatty, sugary food!

**Family and Friends** So crucial for survival. We learned very early on in our evolution that we were better off in groups, tribes, families. We are a social species and need each other to survive and thrive.

**Exercise-Sport** Well, we all need to move to keep our bodies healthy! So whether it is serious marathon type exercise, or simply walking, it is crucial to keep moving. As soon as we don't, our bodies will suffer, our lives shorter.

Not everyone plays a sport, but those that do, get not only the exercise it provides but also social cohesion. Even if we just watch a game or support a team., we "belong" to that group, and we benefit from that.

**Music and dancing** We are a pattern-seeking species, our brains respond to patterns, and there is no more significant example than with music! And of course, we used to sing and dance around campfires, cementing our groups and responding to the feel-good chemicals that music provides.

**Animals and Nature** We have always had a symbiotic relationship with other animals, we have used them for work, transport and sadly to eat! It is well known that we benefit from contact with animals, stroking a dog for example, will release the "cuddle chemical" Oxytocin to both you and the dog!

**Shopping** Some people thoroughly enjoy shopping! Hard to believe that this has anything to do with survival, but it really has! It stems from a time when we were "Hunter-gatherers", we still have that wiring, although we don't have to go hunting any more. These days we use that facility for "hunting" bargains! Some of us may be more on the "gatherer" side of our ancestors, in which case we might have hoards of bags and shoes!

**Senses** Crucial for survival! We have inherited these from our predecessors, and then developed and honed those senses over our lifetimes- for our survival. We should never underestimate them, our sense of smell and hearing sight and touch and taste, are essential skills. We are part of the animal kingdom, after all, and these senses are inherent gems.

So the bottom line is that if something gives us pleasure, we are experiencing Dopamine in the pleasure centre of our brains our brain perceives it as being necessary for our survival! Dopamine is the primary neurotransmitter of the reward pathway.
We have evolved these instincts to encourage avoidance of bad situations and seek out positive ones.

   Beneficial behaviour carries a reward to drive repetition of that behaviour.
      The pleasure centre lives in a fundamental brain area
Its control can be far greater than that of the thinking part of our brain, and so it can easily overpower common sense.

      The drugs of abuse are both "rewarding" and reinforcing" and they "hijack" the brain's natural reward circuitry.
Stimulation of that pathway reinforces the behaviour.
So that ensures that whatever you just did you will want to do it again!
      Drugs create enormous sensations of pleasure and excitement; Instead of a handful of receptors being stimulated, there is an avalanche of neurotransmitter activation. If you consider that sexual intercourse is the greatest "pleasure hit" for human beings, it is hard to believe that all of the substances of misuse have a far greater pleasurable affect, something like crack cocaine, for example is 1,000 times more potent than sex!
So Users very definitely fall in love with the pleasure centre.
      When the drugs are removed, and the brain no longer has the stimulation it has got used to, it perceives itself to be in a life-

threatening situation. Hence withdrawal symptoms and craving to repeat the experience, anxiety, palpitations, insomnia etc.

The rest of the brain cannot be heard in the presence of strong chemicals. Receptors will only be able to "hear" when the drugs are stopped.

How do drugs affect neurotransmitters, and why does it matter anyway?

Neurotransmitters modulate human behaviours and emotions. It works as a "feedback" mechanism, a bit like a thermostat in your heating, or air conditioning. Firstly, the drugs of abuse disturb that delicate balance.

Then tolerance occurs.

If a neurotransmitter is overactive, the neurons "turn down" their sensitivity to that neurotransmitter. If a neurotransmitter is underactive, the neurons "turn up" their sensitivity.

We know that Human beings can cope with change for a while, but not for long, and the drugs of abuse have long term consequences.

So when we look at the regions of the brain which are of particular concern, it helps to first look at how the brain developed and evolved.

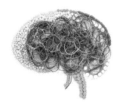

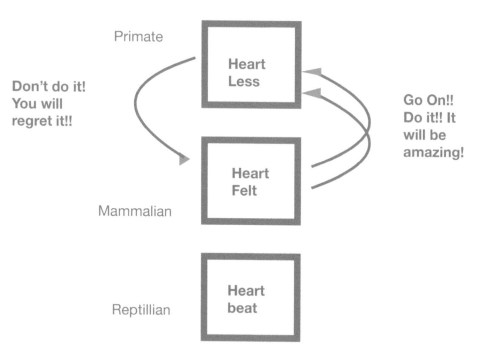

This is referred to as the "Triunal Brain"The first bit to develop was the Brain stem, just above the spinal cord, and often referred to as the "Reptilian" brain". This is the part that deals with unconscious activities like metabolism, respiration, heartbeat etc. Things we don't have to "think" about. We can call this "Heartbeat."

Then a few thousand years later, we developed the next part - the "Limbic system", often referred to as the "Mammalian brain" This is the bit that deals with the unconscious regulation of instinct to carry out survival behaviour. It deals with the regulation of emotions. When talk about feelings, we often say we "feel them in our heart"! Of course, we feel emotions in our brain; our heart is just a pump! So we can call this bit "Heartfelt".

A few thousand more years and we got the last bit- The "Pre-frontal cortex".referred to as the "Primate brain". This is the "sharp and shiny" computer bit of our brain, the bit that makes us do the "harder thing". To enable us to resist temptation. If we want to perform gratification postponement, we need to activate the pre-frontal cortex. But this bit doesn't "feel" anything, so for want of a better word we can call this "Heartless".

Anything that feels good increases Dopamine levels in reward pathways the Limbic system.If there is a degree of excitation in the Limbic system, it has an enormous role in the decisions we make, because it can easily inhibit the pre-frontal cortex.

*Addiction is ALL about emotions!*

You will see there are projections going from the Limbic system, saying "Go on do it it will feel amazing."

At the same time, projections are coming from the pre-frontal cortex saying "Don't do it, you are going to regret it"!

Notice that we are a bit biased towards the "do it" part, to survive. But under normal circumstances, the pre frontal cortex can contain our behaviour, give us enough zealousness to keep us out of mischief!

For many years the only way we could see how the brain worked, was if something went wrong, or when a person was dead. These days with the advent of neural imaging, it is possible to see the real-time workings of the brain when a person is alive.

There was a very famous neuroscience patient, called Phineas Gage, who was a railroad worker in the nineteenth century.

He was a "tamper man", someone who used a "tamper" rod to tamp down dynamite into holes of boulders to blow them up, enabling the railway to be laid.

Phineas was very good at his job, was a good employee, he was married and was a good husband. He had children and was an excellent father.In fact, he was an all-round "good chap".

Then one day, Phineas was a bit "ambitious" with his tamper rod, and the boulder blew up in his face, sending the rod though is cheekbone, out through his head, taking with it his pre-frontal cortex which landed 10 feet away still attached to the tamper rod.

It was miraculous that he didn't die, he was not even rendered unconscious, but was trundled off to the doctors' where he didn't get an infection, nor did he bleed out. However, after this terrible accident,

Phineas was a changed man! He became disinhibited, profane, socially inappropriate. In the doctor's notes, it says "This man is no longer Phineas Gage, and should not be left alone in female company". Poor Phineas lost his job, his wife, his children, his life really ,when he lost his pre-frontal cortex and the ability to restrain his basic urges.
He ended his days as a curiosity in a circus sideshow.

The limbic system can easily inhibit the pre frontal cortex, making things irresistible. This is the physiology of acting on impulse.

Drugs of abuse in the limbic system are a prime example of this.For example, who among us hasn't had "one too many" on occasions? And suddenly you are the best dancer in the club! the greatest karaoke singer! Inhibitions are impaired, or even gone! Perhaps you kissed someone you shouldn't? Maybe went home with someone you shouldn't?

So if the pre-frontal cortex wants to get a look in, we have to calm down the Limbic system!

Important to remember that the pre-frontal cortex doesn't **"feel"** things, and the Limbic system doesn't listen to words!

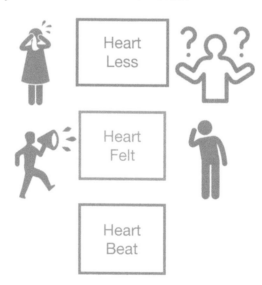

We insist on talking and talking ! but the limbic system cannot hear!It only <u>feels</u> and it is the emotional part of the brain that is struggling.

### *Addiction is ALL about emotions!*

So when we, albeit with the best of intentions, try and "talk" the addict out of their habits, we are pretty much wasting our time! Addicts have heard <u>all</u> of the words, <u>all</u> the arguments, <u>all</u> of the advice.

Addicts are <u>not</u> stupid! Their problem does not lie in lack of intellect or knowledge, but the overwhelming hold that drugs have on their Limbic system! When we are in the grips of our using, the Limbic system is in charge, and it is impervious to words!

I think of a shouting "Limbic system" as a hungry baby wolf. Imagine you are locked in a room with him, and he is eyeing you up for dinner! But you are fortunate, in the room there is a fridge full of meat! So you throw him a piece of meat, and he licks his paws, happy for a while.But then he gets hungry again, and he is coming at you!So you throw him another bit of meat, and that satisfies him for while, then other then another- until your fridge is empty! And now you have a BIG wolf, because you have fed him! If we are to make any headway, we need first stop feeding that beast, calm down the limbic system, so that the rest of the brain can "hear".

We need strategies for that, which is where our "programme" comes in. Supporting whatever other programme you may be using.

## Chapter Six
### Learning

---

**Addiction is defined as the use of an  addictor, a substance, a person, a thought, a feeling or behaviour for purpose of changing how they feel, irrespective of the consequences, against their conscious will.**

So who can become addicted?
Well, indeed anyone can become addicted! But there is no doubt that there are some people who are more prone to addictive behaviour  than others—those with a particular predisposition which has then been "turned on" by life events.

We can put too much blame on the "bad stuff" that has happened to us, not everyone who has experienced, grief, divorce, abuse, etc. inevitably becomes addicted to chemicals.. So we have to concede there must be something different about those of us who are.

We have to ask  why would natural selection allow for this trait to continue? Despite its destructive nature, addiction is still as prevalent as ever, so why would that be so?

It would suggest that there is some kind of biological advantage to having this brain wiring. Which is not something we hear often! Mostly the only things we ever hear are incredibly negative!

Remember, that as human beings, we are designed to seek out rewarding behaviour for survival, we are all seekers of pleasure. And also remember that some of us don't experience that pleasure as easily, we have that sense of ennui, "underwhelmed".So we become even more fervent "seekers"

**Addicts  are like seekers on rocket fuel!**

Natural selection allows some of us to have alleles(types of genes) of low reward activity. In order to feel the same reward as others, we would need a very much stronger stimulus stimulus.This stems from time; for example, when food and water were harder to come by. We needed people with that drive to go out for days on end to find them. They were the ones seeking the biggest boar the fattest kill, and would not be content with the apple tree in the garden!

Although that time is now passed, some of us still have that residual wiring, and still, seek out "higher reward" behaviours. Inevitably, in the absence of a need to find the fattest kill, that drive might lead to chemicals that give us the biggest "hit".

When an addict finds recovery, they still have that hard wiring! It doesn't go away. They will still be very driven people!

In fact, they are precisely the ones you need on your team! They will still be extremely driven, by whatever it is they have found to support them. Often we feel so passionate about our recovery that we find a drive to help others. So you will find many who ultimately go to work in this field.

I think most addicts who have found recovery have compassion for their fellows and a burning desire to pass on their experience, strength and hope. Others become powerful in all kinds of areas. The point is they will be very driven wherever they find their own passions. Once they have regained their power, they will be determined to use it! Having discovered that some people have a predisposition to addiction due to their specialised brain wiring, we should now consider that second "opinion" that this condition is "learned" and look at how we actually learn things.

**Learning** Contrary to popular belief, We don't have a "bag" of memories or information in our heads; there wouldn't be room! What we <u>do</u> have are neurons, and remember they are all in pathways, and those pathways are in regions.

We don't grow new neurons when we learn things, otherwise our heads would be enormous!

The way we we learn, is to strengthen given pathways, thereby making them more potent.

We learn everything in two ways :

The repeated stimulus of a given pathway in the same way we learn to swim or drive: by repetition.

Or incredibly strong stimulation of a given pathway So we are more liable to remember things when there is an emption attached.We tend to remember things that are particularly good or bad, funny sad etc.

Both of these are a factor in addictive behaviour. We have an incredibly strong stimulus AND repetition!

Once a pathway has been strengthened, "Long term potentiation" "LTP" occurs. It its a bit like when you first ski down a slope, before anyone else has skied down it, you don't need to worry too much, it's nice and slow.When a dozen people have been down the same slope however, it will become lethal!Long term potentiation is, as the name suggests a physical change that has permanently changed the pathway. It is terribly difficult to do the harder thing, against an LTP'd pathway. Part of the brain has permanently changed its function, and It has become "Entrained."

**Before learning Not much traffic, a bit slow**

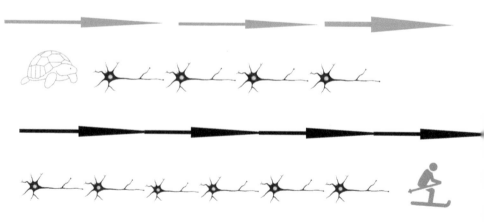

After LTP the pathway is "Entrained"  Like breakneck speed !

With long term potentiation, the brain has learned the experience of profound reward (or terror) and what caused it, and these persistent memories are potentiated.
The drugs themselves will reactivate pathways more intensely due to LTP as do the memories of experiences of trauma.
    This is, of course, how "triggers" occur. It does not always have to be the using of drugs, but even associated triggers like the sight of a hypodermic needle or the pub one used to drink in, or a person, a piece of music etc. This is Pavlovian conditioning.
    It is a suggestion that if we are to become a "master" of anything, we need to practice for at least ten thousand hours.
My husband, Gez, is a drummer. He has been playing since he was very young, and he still practices every day. He is a "master" drummer no doubt, and he is terrific! But it is interesting to see that as an old couple, the pair of us often drop to sleep in front of the television these days!
Gez can be completely unconscious, and world war three could break out, and he wouldn't hear it. But if a piece of music comes on, suddenly you will see his "bass pedal" foot start twitching, then the other, then his hands!
Still fast asleep, Long term potentiation has occurred and is quickly "triggered!" THAT is how incredibly powerful Long Term Potentiation is! It could be said that most of us who have abused chemicals are indeed "masters" at it! Ten thousand hours practice doesn't seem that much!!
    Years ago, we used to believe that brains were static and always stayed the same.We now know that our brains change all through our lives, and we call that neuroplasticity.
We don't acquire new neurons as we learn, but we do create new synaptic connections.
If neurons fire together, they wire together!
This is how "triggers" work

Our brain is doing this all the time, looking, listening for things we recognise, for our survival.

Millions of images are bombarding our brains every second,.

If someone takes or even thinks about a substance, the brain will reactivate the entrained pathway, and the addictive cycle can quickly retake a firm hold. So we see people who have been abstinent for year suddenly return to using, because they have been "triggered" in some way.

As we've seen, learning is very much linked to our emotions. So if we have used chemicals when we are tired, sad hurt, lonely or afraid, our brain has "learned" that connection and then the minute we feel those emotions again, the addictive cycle can be set in motion.

There's no doubt, the implications for this are massive! And really should NOT be underestimated. And it means one thing:

Once an addict, always an addict! You cannot go back

That doesn't mean you can't get well and become empowered, but it does mean that you have to change! 更改, 变化

Inside each one of us are two wolves
fighting

One is full of
Anger
Greed
Regret
Envy
Arrogance
Inferiority
Self Pity
Guilt
Resentment
Lies
Superiority
Ego

One is full of
Love
Hope
Humility
Kindness
Honour
Joy
Empathy
Serenity
Benevolence
Truth
Compassion
Honesty

Which one wins? — The One you feed the most!

## Chapter Seven
### Epigenetics 表觀遺傳學

---

All of us are a sum total of our genetic predispositions and our life experiences. Epigenetic's is the way that our life experiences change things.The prefix"epi" means "on", "near", "over" "above". There is a saying that:

**"Genes load the gun, and Epigenetic's pull the trigger"!**

Every single thing that has happened to us makes us who we are. Every interaction, every experience, every conversation, every bit of learning. And that change is physical.

Genes are not static, and they are a predisposition, not a pre-determination. Genes can be "turned on" by life experiences or even drugs themselves. Also, modifications to DNA can occur in response to life events. This contributes to the addicted brain, to craving and sensitisation of drug cues.

Every single thing that we have ever learned changes our brains physically; that is how learning occurs. As we saw when we discussed **"Long term Potentiation"**.
we can't look for our memories in those neural pathways, our memories ARE the pathways which have been changed and potentiated.

There is no doubt that there are some experiences that have a more profound effect on us.especially those we experience when we are young, and our brains are still malleable.

Genes themselves do not change because of those life events, instead, what happens is that specific proteins attached to the gene referred to as a "marker" which changes the way the gene expresses itself. Once again we are focusing on "shape", if it changes shape then the gene will behave in a different way. Hence the person will function differently.

Epigenetic Marker

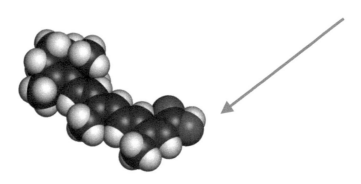

**Adverse Childhood Experiences.**

These events that are referred to as "ACE" s"

It is clear that we already have an understanding that what happens to our children might affect them later in life. Why else would we try and create a safe and nurturing environment for them? if it didn't matter, we wouldn't bother.

So it is hardly surprising to learn that these "adverse childhood experiences" are toxic and can last a lifetime.

They are many and various, they can take the form of things like:
*Abuse or neglect.
*Having a family member who is mentally ill or addicted.
*Experiencing, or even witnessing domestic violence.

*Having a parent in prison.
*Losing a parent to divorce or separation.
*Being bullied, by a peer or adult.
*Losing a family member.

**There can be adverse community experiences:**
*Living in a war zone.
*Living in an unsafe environment.

**Adverse Climate experiences:**
*Being involved in a natural disaster, flood, earthquake, Tsunami.
*These can even be historic stresses, like living in a situation where there has previously been turmoil and having parents, grandparents who have experienced that trauma and have sustained  epigenetic changes.

All of these experiences can cause  "toxic" stress. That can damage brain development, create susceptibility to short and long term health problems: immune system diseases, heart disease, cancer, and changes to DNA.
So we should never underestimate what people have gone through, to bring them to where they are now. Those adverse experiences aren't an excuse for destructive behaviour, but they are an explanation.

童年不辛經歷

## So let's recap.

*Our beloved addicted person has specialised "hard wiring", and the innate drive for "Bigger Better, More".
That biological advantage which would have been invaluable in years gone by, is now a biological challenge.

Hence that genetic predisposition towards addiction.That wiring cannot be reversed, but can be powerful when harnessed.

*We may have  experienced some of the "ACE's "- life events that "turn on" that gene expression.
It is said that if a human being experiences four Adverse Childhood experiences, their life path may well be changed.
In my experience, most of us have experienced far far more!

*As we've seen, there will entrained neural pathways, because of Long term potentiation.

*We then find  very powerful ,addictive, and toxic  YANG chemicals, and our chaotic Yang behaviour deteriorates  as we  chase that illusive "satisfaction"

*We have depleted SEROTONIN which could provide that satiation.It is that inability of serotonin which is often neglected.

Then it is hardly surprising that they now may  follow a destructive path
 Of course there will be amends to make, and perhaps charges to answer, but  it is crucial that we make our recovery  THE most important thing in our lives, without it we will surely have nothing.

The challenge is to address imbalances, rather than focus on the using behaviour alone.
Abstinence is the imperative.

Once those entrained pathways have been created, they cannot be reversed, They will be always there.

It is difficult to do the harder thing against a Long term potentiated pathway, and mood altering chemicals will quickly recreate their strong hold again.
But we can strengthen new neural pathways so they will become favoured.

A thorough understanding of the brain and that pre disposition will be good starting point.

The challenge then is to calm down the Limbic System allowing the pre-frontal cortex to get stronger.

We need then to Increase Serotonin.

We will offer some ideas on how this can all be achieved in the chapter about our "Five Star recovery" programme.

**But I reiterate!: We are NOT broken or flawed, sick or morally weak!! We are simply wired in a way that would have been a valuable trait in years gone by. We still have that rocket fuel and an extraordinary ability to soar! And reach for the stars!**

## Chapter Eight

### "5 Star" Wellbeing Programme

---

.        Our 5-star wellbeing programme is not specifically about acupuncture, although it does draw a lot on some on its wonderful Chinese theories. It has also borrowed other words of wisdom from a variety of sources! Not least from every amazing addict in recovery that I have met in 45 years!!

It's based on two "Fives": the "Five-element" theory, that underpins much of Chinese thought, and the idea that anything considered "5 Star" is the very best!!

When I first started my own recovery, I was often told that everything I needed was "within me"! I didn't know what the hell they were talking about! I was utterly powerless, and had very little faith in anything the was "within me"! Of course, it was quite true, but no one really told me what it was that was "within me" I had to find out for myself!

I had to go right back to the very beginning, not my beginning, but the Universe! Right back to the "Big Bang" and the formation of the atoms that make me and everything else. It resonated with me, knowing that I was made of stardust! As human beings, we are all made of the very same "stardust" So nurturing and strengthening that "stardust" seemed to make sense! Regardless of whether we are using any other programme or none at all, we will need "fuel" for that undertaking!

We do forget I think, that we are all part of nature, and as such, have some powerful natural skills! We tend to dismiss them in our search for a new pill or a magic wand, and we definitely take them for granted, but they have kept us alive for millennia, and are still a part of our remaining alive.

**Our sight and hearing, senses of smell, touch and taste are incredible survival abilities.**

Ours is a wellbeing programme that anyone can use—a way of accessing and honing those extraordinary inherent abilities that as humans, we all possess.

I have often been asked why we don't teach auricular acupuncture to just anybody who might be "interested" in our training, perhaps other "complementary therapists" or family members. Our stance on this has been the source of annoyance to some.

We decided early on that anybody we taught this treatment to should have a professional understanding of substance misuse or mental health conditions, in some capacity. The formulae treatment we teach is not a stand-alone treatment or a magic bullet.It needs to be used in conjunction with other interventions.

Addiction is not only very complicated, but it is also life-threatening. Far more people die from its impact than ever recover, which is a sobering and distressing fact.

We have observed some people, with no other skills, treating this treatment as a party trick. Equally sadly, often qualified acupuncturists naive in their attitude, believe that their kindness and therapy will "cure" a hardened addict. They imagine that "kindness" is what is missing, but families will tell you they have tried everything, from kindness to threats, to no avail.

There are far too many addicts who have been killed with kindness! We decided that by stipulating that those we teach should already be employed in this field in some capacity or other, we were safeguarding the vulnerable patient group and preserving the traditional acupuncture profession's holistic nature.

We didn't want to create a sort of "subculture" therapy that might endanger the addict. People must understand the boundaries and limitations of this treatment.

We have heard every argument about that! Some have said, "it is better than nothing", but we disagree, while a patient is getting a "better than nothing" treatment, they might be steadily deteriorating.

Addiction has always been the "Cinderella" of healthcare priorities, and we don't want to perpetuate that attitude. I believe that everyone should expect the very "BEST BIGGEST MOST"!

In the time we have spent teaching our programme, we have always strived to offer the very best experience.
I have a rule that the one person who we need always prioritise, is the man in the "empty chair". It represents the person asking for help, maybe even dying. Sometimes I have even put an empty chair in meetings to remind us what our focus should be. Every time we change anything or consider something new, we need to imagine that person in the empty chair and how our actions may benefit or even damage him. .I believe that if my focus is always on the patient and his wellbeing, then I can't go too far wrong.

BUT! That does not mean I don't teach the "5-star wellbeing" programme to others; in fact, I am thoroughly engaged in doing just that! Optimum brain health is vital for everyone, as is our general health, and this approach is a great way to enhance it.

Ever since we have been teaching professionals in this field, I have felt a huge "hunger" for the chance to deliver our discoveries to addicts themselves.

Addicted people are NOT stupid! Moreover, I disapprove of the "power imbalance" created in some services—the disempowerment of the client who has at that stage been stripped of any sense of agency. I have relished the chance to teach prisoners our empowering "5-star wellbeing programme".

For this "5 Star" wellbeing approach, I draw again, on my Chinese medicine background. Some of those beautiful analogies, which explain complicated systems.

This time I am focusing particularly on the Five Element theory.

五行學說(中醫

The FiveElement theory is one of the fundamental theories in Chinese thought. Along with the Yin Yang theory, it is used in Chinese medicine diagnosis and treatment. It is a beautiful and somewhat poetic analogy to describe complicated systems of the `Universe in a simple way. And is there for everyone, not solely for a Chinese medical practitioner.So please use it!

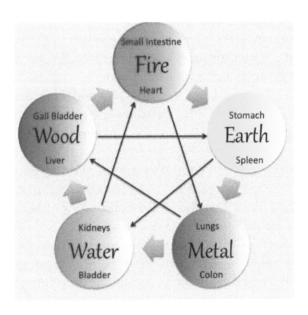

We can look at anything in the Universe as appertaining to the five elements: this is about the nature of being human and an essential part of the Universe.

As Human Beings, we are very much part of nature and subject to natural laws. Sometimes we forget this because we can build houses for shelter, and we can go to the supermarket for a tin of peas, we no longer have to be "Hunter-Gatherers".

As we are part of that same nature, it is considered that we have all of the five elements within us. As a practitioner, one of my first jobs would be to determine which of these elements is my patient's predominant one, A sort of "signature" element.

This is nothing like a horoscope or anything mystical if anything it pertains more to our DNA!

Here we are talking about nurturing ALL of the elements, rather than singling one out, which takes fairly complicated individual diagnosis. In the absence of knowing which one is most prominent, it makes sense to nurture ALL of them!

You already know about the five-element stuff! You may not have known the words, or have learned the theories, but we ALL do know it! This is our innate energetic "language" and is all about our survival. A bit like body language, it is not something we had to learn. The terminology sounds a little weird, to begin with, not our everyday language but we all have this fundamental intuitive understating.

Therefore, my aim with this programme is to show how we can reconnect with, and nurture those five elements within ourselves, and show others how they too can aim for optimum well-being by strengthening the five elements.

Each element has qualities and vulnerabilities. Each one has associations: a sound, a taste, a colour, time of year, an emotion, a smell, strengths, and weaknesses. Absolutely everything in the Universe appertains to one or other of these elements. By understanding each one, and with a combination of the five senses, diet, meditation, connections with others, acupressure, acupuncture, nutrition, etc. we can show how we can support the restoration of our potential.

The five-element theory describes the way the ancient Chinese viewed and explained the entire Universe. They began by looking at the seasons, recognising that the energy at different times in the year was also changed.

(Unlike in the West, the Chinese recognised five seasons rather than four, and the one they add is called "Late Summer" That beautiful time here in between August and September, which is not the full burst of Summer, but certainly isn't Autumn yet. It is "Harvest time" The Chinese see"Late Summer" as a season in its own right, represented in the Earth element.)

# WOOD 木

**Wood** (In terms of Chinese medicine, the Wood element is associated with the Liver and Gall bladder, but that is not what we are concerned with here.)

The **Wood** element is associated with the Springtime, that vibrant time of birth and new growth.

Think of the energy in Springtime, it is very volatile, upward energy, the kind that is strong enough to push a blade of grass through something as hard as concrete! It is a time too of change, and the weather in this season is often windy, perhaps where we get the saying "The winds of change.

The sound associated with **Wood** is "shouting" the emotion is **"Anger"** the sense related to **Wood** is **"Vision"**.

**Wood** is associated with **Creativity, Posture,Structure, Boundaries, and PlansWOOD**

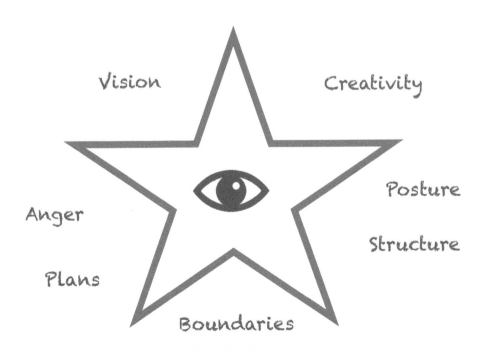

So it is easy perhaps to see how we can begin to nurture this element:
We can strive to have a **structure** in our day, have plans both for the
day and long term. We can strengthen our **boundaries**, learn to say
**"No"** make sure we are not allowing others to push our boundaries.
We can start to improve our **posture**, perhaps we never think
about it much, thinking about it more mindfully will improve it.
A great way to use posture to our advantage is with the "Winning"
posture:
Our brain is incredibly clever, but it doesn't always know when
we are trying to fool it! So it will often respond to physical cues that are
actually "fake."

If you watch Someone who has just won something, got a gold
medal they usually adopt this "winning" position.

If we put our bodies into this position, and "act as if", then our
brain will send those "feel good" chemicals, in the same way as a real
win!
So I suggest that you do this **five** minutes before an important
meeting, an interview or parole board, in fact anytime you want to feel
more like **"Winner"**! Do it sometime during every day! Stretching is
also a good "plan" so stretch your body **five** times in the day!

## Creativity

We do all have a "creative" side; for some, it seems more developed than others, but we can all nurture that part of us daily to support the **Wood** element.

You might like to draw or paint, bake or write poetry or songs, or even just put a daffodil in a milk bottle! I cannot draw at all, but I live with a very accomplished artist, I appreciate what he does, just watching him work will feed my **Wood** element .But I <u>can</u> bake cakes, and I love having flowers around. Make **creativity** a part of the plan for your day.

The emotion associated with Wood is **"ANGER"**. We know how destructive this particular emotion can be. But it can also be useful when we want to bring about changes. I doubt we would have been able to change anything that was unfair through history unless we were angry about it. Someone needed to get angry about injustice, slavery, inequality, and abuse.
**Anger,** however, can blind us to anything positive if it is left to go untethered, think about being in a "**blind rage.**"
It can be so blinding that we can't see "the wood for the trees

So it is better to explain our anger rather than express it, and deal with it straight away while it is small, and before it becomes huge and blinding.
The sense associated with Wood is **"Vision"**. All of our senses are our specialised survival skills, honed over millennia; Our eyes are processing billions of images a second to keep us safe by spotting danger, and to seek out pleasurable images.

It is l as important today as it was in our earlier evolution, to be able to see our way around the world.
We can call on this sense to lift our spirits ,and ,at the same time, strengthening it to serve us better.

I suggest we find at least **five** images that make us feel good when we look at them. It could be our kids or partners, maybe a view of the sea, flowers, or mountains or whatever lifts **YOUR** spirits.

Once again, we can call upon our brain's desire to make us feel good. Research has shown that one of the images that make people feel especially good, and make the brain send those beneficial chemicals, is being in dappled light, as the sun comes through the tree canopy.

I know we can't all be under the trees, but the research also suggests that just looking at a picture of dappled light has pretty much the same effect! So make that one of your **FIVE** pictures!

We can put our **five** images on our smartphones. But in the absence of a phone, cut the pictures out of magazines and maybe stick them where you can see them. You can have as many as you like, but make sure you have at least **five**!

Going "outside" will nurture the **WOOD** element, getting back to nature in some way. Fresh air is great for wellbeing, and there are "pictures" to see all over in the natural world.

It has been shown that putting hands in the soil; <u>any</u> soil is good for us! That is not just "hippy" thinking, and there is research to prove it!

There is a bacteria in soil, **"Mycobacterium vaccae"** which has been shown to increase Serotonin! So get your hands in the dirt! Even a plant pot or a window box, or if the opportunity arises, walk barefoot on the grass

Exercising is always beneficial, But doing as much of it outside as you can, is even more helpful. Nurture the WOOD element every day but being outside, regardless of the weather, for at least twenty minutes Being outside, boosts your energy, helps reduce blood pressure and stress, boosts your immune system, enhances creativity There is free aromatherapy and visual images to lift your spirits Increases Serotonin!

And remember any activity that we can do with others is doubly beneficial. So go for a walk with someone else.

# FIRE

火 **Fire**( In Chinese medicine, we consider the Fire element
is concerned with the heart, small intestines, the triple burner, which is a
bit like our "central heating" and the pericardium, but that isn't what we
are concerned with here)

The Fire element is concerned with the Summertime. That time
of "blossoming" of "outward" energy, the kind that sees flowers and
plants "opening up" embracing the warmth and light, even human
beings tend to "open out" in the Summer, we increase our surface area
to stay cool.

The Fire element is very much about people: relationships, love,
warmth, communication. It is about fun and humour, and so you can see
why the emotion associated with Fire is joy. The sense is Taste.

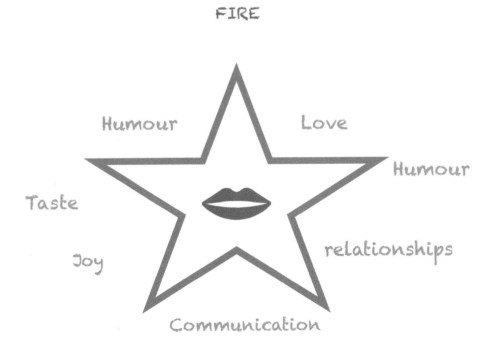

**Fire** is so much about "people"-There's no doubt that the people in our lives can be of great benefit and a source of joy.
They can also be a big part of our problems! Our relationships with people are very much part of our lives.
If we want to thrive, it is essential as a human being to be part of a "pack", a tribe, a family a team. Our ancestors realised this a long time ago. The necessity for cooperation with others has been crucial in the survival of our species.
So it easy to see how when we have been "isolated" or alienated, it is detrimental to our wellbeing.
Often this is the case with those of us who have been addicted or abused. We will have had awful experiences with others. Our "trust" mechanisms may be shot. Sometimes our behaviour has also been alienating.
Whatever the reason, we need to find a way of being part of a pack of creating a "team."
This is where "recovery groups" can often be beneficial; they might be our first venture into reconnecting with other humans. After starting small, we may then feel like widening our circles a bit. There are recovery groups all over the place, find one that you feel comfortable with. It does not have to be AA or NA, although one of the benefits of the twelve-step programme is its anonymity, so you can try out being with people with no strings!

五個要素 I especially draw on the five-element theory again to help
with finding a supportive team!
Think of **five** people in your life, or who you would like to have around
you-
Someone who will "make you laugh", Someone who will "care for
you." Someone "You are inspired by", Someone who will
"reassure" you,
and Someone who will "fight your corner."
They may be real people, and already part of your life or they may be
"superheroes" that you would like to be part of your team! Once again,
get the images, have them near you. Here is the team that is going to be
part of your restoration!
Your Five element allies

Surround yourself with people with these qualities, but make sure you have at least FIVE!
There's a wonderful Native American saying which is good for us all to use:

"Find your tribe and love them hard!"

Talking is important, but if it is challenging to communicate with someone, consider doing it a different way, write a letter, send an email, make a Zoom call, take part in a group of some kind. Show your willingness to connect. Trying to mend broken relationships is a challenge, but it may make help long term restoration. If you have to have an awkward conversation, it may be useful to practice it beforehand.
Take good care of your "heart"; don't put yourself into a place where you may get hurt.

Sometimes this might mean getting rid of toxic relationships! Don't think you have to stay around people who bring you down.I have a "rule of thumb" when thinking about relationships with people. I ask myself"does this relationship nourish me in any way?" and if the answer is "No" then I walk away from it!
I find talking to my dog is especially therapeutic! Lots of "unconditional love"! If you don't have one, try talking to somebody else's, or even the cows in the field! Start practicing your communication skills!

We know that **Humour** is one of the best medicines around; it helps so many things. You know that if you see something funny, you will have a giggle, you will get those "feel-good chemicals".
If you see something funny when you are with others, you will have a real "belly laugh" and so even more feel-good chemicals!
Humans, like all other primates (all mammals), are focused on what we see. We always needed to know who was a friend or foe, a predator or prey!
Smiling, and other non-verbal cues show acceptance, kindness and even if it's in
passing on a corner with a stranger, the gift
of acceptance. It is essential for
communication. Try smiling at everyone you
meet, a genuine smile with good eye
contact.
Determine to smile as much as you can, and laugh often - at least five times a day! Give it away too, a smile is contagious!! Pass it on.
We know that smiling is good for us, our brain floods with those chemicals, but what we also know is the brain can be fooled! So if you just put your facial muscles in the shape of a smile, you will get the same effect! So fake it until you make it!
Cut out a "smiley" picture and look at it often, or have one
on your phone to remind you!

The sense associated with Fire is Taste. The sense of taste has also helped our evolution and survival.
It helped us test the food we were about to eat. Something salty our sweet may have meant that it had were plenty of nutrients, whereas a bitter or sour taste suggested the food may be rotten or poisonous.

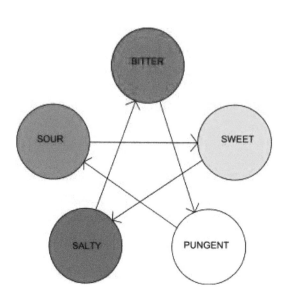

So think of the tastes you prefer. That doesn't mean overindulging on junk; this is not about "diet" so much as "taste".

Think about what tastes you like, and make sure you have your favourite tasting things around you for times when you need them. It might be sour things like lemons, bitter things like coffee or chicory; it will be personal to you.

Think of five tastes that you love, keep them near! I particularly like lemon flavoured things, and "crisp" things like crackers or apples, so I always have them around, "just in case"! maybe you love salty things or sweet, they will be your personal likes.

## Earth 土（中醫

In Chinese medicine we consider the Earth element to be concerned with the stomach and spleen, but that is not what we are concerned with here)
The Earth element is concerned with "Late Summer" that extra season that the Chinese give to our calendar! It is that beautiful time of year somewhere between August and September, which is not really the full blaze of Summer, but it certainly isn't Autumn yet.
It is a golden time of abundance, lots of produce, "Harvest time." The energy around late Summer is quite "still."
The Earth element is concerned with Nurturing, Caring, Compassion, Movement. The emotion associated with Earth is Sympathy, and the sense for Earth is Touch.

EARTH

So when considering the                    "nurturing" aspect of
Earth, we might begin by thinking of diet, what kinds of foods make us
feel our best.
Over the years we have often been asked: "What is the best diet" and
there are whole libraries of books about that subject!
Many people have their own "pet diet". and I am sure they all have
merit, depending on why you may be using them. I think an excellent "
all-round" approach is to "eat a rainbow a day."
Getting as many colours on your plate as possible. Each different colour
has specific nutrients associated with it, so even if you don't know a
whole lot about nutrition, it is a great way to get all of those different
nutrients.
By and large, in this country, we tend to use too many "supplements."
We are bombarded with adverts about them, from cod liver oil to Zinc!
And it is big business, from "buy one get one for a penny" to emotive
ways of protecting your children. It is a minefield, especially when
these companies prey on our desire to stay well and keep our families
well.
In this "ideal world" that most of us don't live in, the best way to get the
nutrition we need is with a healthy balanced diet.
There's no doubt the best way to get your vitamins and minerals is to eat
them. Sadly, for so many reasons, we don't always get a balanced diet,
maybe we work shifts, eat "on the hoof" even because our food can be
lacking in proper nutrition because of chemicals, processing, etc.

When I was a child, we said that we should have "Apple a day
to keep the doctor away". I am told that these days, I would
need to eat TEN apples to get the same nutritional value!
Very worrying to think of what we may have done to the
humble apple!

There may be times when a nutritional supplement is needed, maybe to support a specific condition, or after illness etc. but it is vital to be careful of that "minefield".
The "rule of thumb" here is always to make sure you are only supplementing that which you are deficient in- it is unnecessary to have multiple vitamins and minerals that aren't deficient. You will only use that which you need; the rest are excreted, so your hard- earned money is being flushed away!
The other rule is only to use GOOD quality supplements, those that are in a "food state". If, for example, you had a deficiency in Vitamin B. There is no doubt that if you go to a cheap health food supplier, there will be vitamin B in the pot. What won't be there, however, are the enzymes and co-vitamins you would need to absorb that B vitamin, and so you may only absorb about 20 per cent!
"Food state" supplements mean they are complete with the other things needed for absorption. They are more expensive of course, but you will get what you pay for and perhaps won't need them for long. I only recommend three supplement companies, and so if you need that information, then please do get in touch. There are specific foods that will help recovery so a few tips:

Eat foods rich in Tryptophan - a precursor for Serotonin, which we kn ow need to increase!
The foods rich in Tryptophan are:

Pumpkin and squash seeds Sunflower seeds
Soya foods
Turkey
Fish, shellfish, Oats, Brussel sprouts

Also, it is a good idea to make sure you get enough Magnesium, often referred to as the "Morale mineral." Essential for mental health, and easily destroyed by chemicals.
A deficiency in Magnesium is often the cause of cramps and restless legs.

Foods rich in Magnesium are:
Dark leafy vegetables
Nuts and seeds, especially Brazil nuts and Almonds. Squash and
pumpkin seeds
Fish,
Beans and Lentils
Avocados
Whole grains
Bananas and dried fruit.

A good way of dealing with cramps would be a handful of Epsom salts
in a bath.Epsom salts are Magnesium sulphate.

B vitamins are essential for good mental health as well as Zinc.
Foods rich in B vitamins are:
Whole grains (brown rice, barley, millet) Meat (red meat , poultry,
fish)
Eggs and dairy products (milk , cheese) Legumes ( bananas , lentils)
Seeds and Nuts (sunflower seeds, almonds) Dark leafy vegetables
(broccoli, spinach, kale) Fruits (citrus fruits , avocados ,bananas)

Zinc is an important mineral and cannot be stored, so you need to make
sure you get a right daily amount. It is vital for all health but
particularly mental health, for healing and for the immune system.It is
also essential for men's health.
Foods rich in Zinc are;
meat,
seafood,
nuts,
seeds, (pumpkin and squash seeds) legumes
Eggs
dairy.,
whole grains
and even dark chocolate!

Add these Super "Brain foods" to your diet !
Almonds,are thought to increase blood flow to the brain.
Walnuts are rich in Omega 3
Blueberries, help improve learning and motor skills,
Brussel Sprouts are rich in tryptophan, essential for converting to Serotonin
Ginger is Anti-inflammatory and may help protect brain disease.
Cabbage and Cauliflower are cruciferous which is thought to lower risk of brain and other diseases
Pine Nuts help stimulate brain activity
Apples, Watermelons Melons, target brain function.
Chia seeds are rich in Omega 3
Equally it is good to avoid those foods that have a negative effect on your brain:
Sugary drinks,
Refined carbs, like sugars, white flour processed grains.
Foods high in Trans fats
Highly processed foods
Aspartame used as an artificial sweetener

An excellent way of getting some of these nutrients and also help cravings is with our Smart-UK snacks! Great for anyone, and you can make them up yourselves!
We mix Sunflower seeds which are rich in tryptophan and B vitamins, including Thiamine and folic acid.
Pumpkin Seeds are very rich in Zinc.
Chopped Brazil nuts, which are rich in Selenium, a potent anti-oxidant and mood enhancer. I toast the seeds to release the nutrients and improve the taste.This is a great little snack with so many benefits.

And then there is FISH!
If your Granny told you that fish was "brain food" she was absolutely right! Fish is the preferred protein for the brain. Protein is needed for making neurotransmitters, so very important stuff!
If you don't eat fish, then you really should take a supplement of Omega 3.

If you are vegan, then perhaps substitute that with a Flaxseed supplement.
The Earth element is concerned with Movement, so anything that exercises the body and mind helps nourish Earth.

The "Gym" type exercises are great, of course, and the so-called "enlightened" exercises like Yoga and Tai Chi are beneficial. But the very best exercise for the brain is Walking!
It is thought that even three sedate walks a week will delay dementia.

We used to walk everywhere back in the day, but now it seems we have to add it as some kind of "hobby"! We are designed to walk! So get out and walk more. Sometimes theres a "stuckness" that takes the form of "ruminating" we go over and over the "same old same old "thinking.While ever we ruminate, we are not taking any kind of action! So get out of that ruminating by doing something physical, even running on the spot for a few minutes, and the brain will follow.

## Herbal Infusions

 You may have heard this called detox" tea. I dislike the use of the word "detox"for anything other than a medical detox; it is misleading and incorrect.But these herbal infusions do have great benefits. We call the main one "Recovery Tea"
Some ingredients that were previously used, we thought were inappropriate for this  patient group-peppermint, for example. While peppermint is an excellent herb and has cooling properties, it has the habit of cooling us down by making us sweat, and our patient group cannot afford to sweat anymore that they are already doing!
So we created some herbal infusions to help. They are all western herbs, and each one has beneficial properties.

## Recovery tea

Chamomile- sedative and anti-spasmodic
Skullcap, - Sedative, anti-inflammatory, ant-hypertensive. Catnip-Sedative
Rosemary-Sedative, antibacterial.
Elderflower-supports the respiratory system, sedative. Lime Flowers-Binds to the same receptor site as Benzodiazepines, sedative.
Hops-sedative
This mix is a delightful and beneficial infusion. One heaped teaspoon in boiling Water, infuse to taste. Drink it often. We have also created a "Sleep Tea" So many people find recovery so tricky because of their lack of sleep.
I am not a great fan of Valerian, which is the herb usually suggested for insomniacs. I find it gives me a "sleep hangover." I prefer to use this infusion which is a pleasant sleep-inducing drink, without the side effects.

## Sleep Tea.
Lime Flowers -Binds to the same receptor site as Benzodiazepines,
sedative.
Lavender -Sedative
Lemon Balm - Sedative
Chamomile - Sedative
Passiflora - Sedative
Red Clover Blossom - Sedative.

One heaped teaspoon in boiling Water, infuse to taste, drink a mugful
half an hour before bed.

The sense associated with the Earth element is Touch.
As human beings, we need to touch and be touched. Babies
who are not touched, hugged, or held don't grow well, and can even die.
Touch is thought to be the first sense that we develop,It sends messages
to the brain through neurons in the skin which respond to things like
pressure, light touch, temperature, vibration and pain. We also react to
texture and it can even influence the decisions we make.So don't
underestimate this sense, it is there for your survival!

I don't suggest that we go around "touching" everyone, that might be
misconstrued! And as an abuse survivor, I know it took me years to stop
being suspicious of touch. So I am aware that many people even fear
physical contact.
When I went to Acupuncture college, it was recommended that we
always hug our patients as they left; I was however, uncomfortable with
this practice t, and so were a lot of patients! Be careful who you allow
in your personal space!
Permission is the key, ask if it OK to hug, don't presume!
You may be doing more harm than good and triggering a
terrible experience.
But under normal circumstances, and with safety, there is
nothing more comforting than a hug! I think we should aim for at least
five hugs a day! If you can't do that, then aim for five handshakes!

Stroking an animal has the same effect. When you pet a dog, for example, you get a lovely injection of Oxytocin, often referred to as the "cuddle" chemical! The dog gets some too, so you both benefit!

Perhaps start with making sure you have a good handshake. It is so, sometimes the first contact you have with the other person, so Make handshakes matter!

Firm grip, but don't crush,
No limp "fish fingers"!
Don't hold on too long, or let go too early- about 3 seconds is a good time.Good eye contact.
Smile!
We can nurture the Earth element with things that we touch. Years ago, we might have handled "worry beads.", some cultures still use something similar. Babies often have a particular blanket that comforts them.
Think about the things you like the feel of; it may be a piece of velvet or silk, a smooth pebble, think how much we like popping "bubble wrap"! We often use our "Aromadough", especially for this purpose.
There may be things you hate the feel of, quite
Often when I have been teaching I find people who cannot bear the touch of cotton wool! It sets their teeth on edge!So avoid things you don't want to touch.
Find FIVE things you do like the feel of, and keep them near you;

perhaps in your pocket or handbag, you never know when you are going to need a bit of comfort.

Compassion as associated with the Earth element. But it is essential, to begin with, "self" compassion, not to be confused with self-pity! Self-compassion is really about cutting yourself a bit of slack, being kind to yourself.

I love the Danish concept of "Hygge" pronounced "Hooger." It is all about "self-soothing." Doing things for yourself to make you feel better. It is not some kind of new-age idea; it is part of Danish culture and is engrained in peoples daily lives. I like to think of it as metaphorically wrapping a warm blanket around myself and saying "There There"!

Think of the advice given by air stewards when they tell you to "Put your own life jacket on before you attempt to help someone else."Then you can be of more use to others.

Remember though that you get more feel-good chemicals by helping someone else, compassion is the key!
Nurturing the right part of us is essential for our new way of being.The more we nurture the parts of us that we want to grow the more of those new neural pathways we will strengthen..

# METAL

金 （中醫） **METAL** (In Chinese medicine this element is concerned with the Lungs and the Large Intestine, but that is not what we are concerned with there)

It is about beauty, values, and inspiration. The Metal element is associated with the Autumn, that beautiful
time of falling leaves and bonfires. Think of the energy in Autumn. It is very downward energy, where we see things "dying"
In fact, the Chinese view the Autumn as the season of grief.
In the Autumn we can often feel melancholy, or reflective .
It is a time too of change, leaves are falling off the trees, and there is rain coming down.
Although the weather in this season is often wet, we do have beautiful crisp Autumn days which are filled with lovely colours and smells, sounds of leaves being kicked around.
The sound associated with Metal is "weeping", and the emotion is grief.
The taste is **"pungent"** which is like things that taste spicy or the odour is **putrid,** which sounds unpleasant but is really like the smell of wet leaves, or the damp forest floor.
**Metal** is associated with **"Higher Self"**, **Spirituality, Inspiration,BeautyValues. Altruism, breathing,** and the sense related to **Metal** is **Smell.**

**Metal**

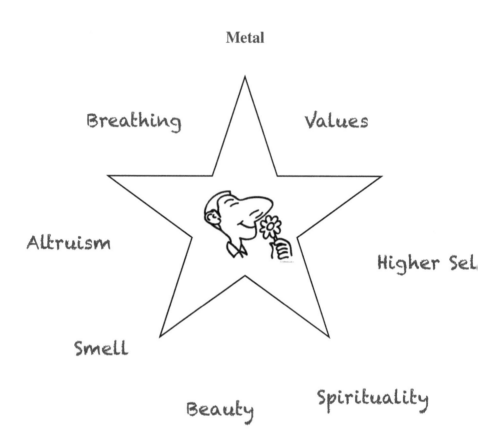

Breathing

Values

Altruism

Higher Sel

Smell

Beauty

Spirituality

**Values** We all have something that is most important to us, whether that is family or faith, profession or a skill of some kind. Nurture those things. To nurture the metal element, we might spend a little more time on that which is most important to us, the most valuable - You are important!

**Beauty**. Make your space, no matter how small, as beautiful as you
canAnywhere can be enhanced, but make sure it is your own choice on
beauty.
Put your best "face" forward, make sure you look as good as you can,
even if there is only you to see you!
Begin to value yourself differently; you are NOT defective and are
made of the same stardust as even the famous and wealthy.

**Altruism** .When we look around us or listen to the news we can hardly
believe that we, as humans, are a benevolent species! But it is true, we
fare very well when we are helping others, we have evolved to be
collaborative, we learned how important we are to each other thousands
of years ago.We often forget it, but we would not have survived this far
as a species without concern for each other.
If someone gives us a gift, theres no doubt we get some of those
wonderful "feel good" chemicals, the person has thought about us,
wanted to make us happy and we are! But if we are the givers- then we
get even more of those feel-good chemicals! We
can feel high as a kite because we something.It is often referred to as
"Helpers High" So if you want to feel good -
do something for someone else!

Even if you can't do
anything else, give someone a compliment. Getting an unexpected
compliment is like a gift, they will get as much of a buzz as if they had
found Ten quid! And you get even more of a Buzz!

Try and do something for someone else without them knowing
about it too! You might pay for someone's coffee in a cafe, or renew
their parking ticket. Put a few coins into a charity box or pick up some
litter, all good spirit lifting stuff.

MeditationYou might think of meditation as something only
for Buddhist monks. But anyone can benefit from meditation. Even
when you take the "religious" connotations out of it, there is extensive
research to show that our brains benefit greatly from meditation
practice.

The brains of seasoned meditators in PET scans are shown to have a
calmer limbic system and a greater developed Pre- frontal cortex. So
what's to lose!!
There are many meditation practices; I particularly like this one that our
friend Richard created just for us!.

## "5 Star" Meditation
### INTRODUCTION

I discovered mediation many years ago, and I have found it an invaluable part of my recovery.

I love the word "refuge", and that is often talked about in meditation practice. I was someone who desperately needed, and yet could not find "refuge' anywhere. It was only when I started to understand meditation practice that I found that elusive place of safety.

For many people, the idea of meditation conjures up Eastern mysticism or particular religious practice. While it is true that there are philosophies that have a meditation practice at their heart, it is also true that it has been proven to have genuine benefits, especially within the brain.

The idea of mindfulness is not new, Monks and others have been practicing it for millennia, it is a shame it has been cynically hijacked in recent years and made a cliche. It is so worthwhile to cultivate, and regular practice will establish new brain patterns.

This simple meditation has been devised especially for us by Richard, an established and experienced meditation teacher who has taught me a lot. This comes as a gift from him, to all suffering beings, and I for one, will practice this daily.

**Contemplations for suffering beings-in other words all of us!**

First settle your body in a comfortable but balanced upright position.Take a few deep, calming breaths.
You may have as one of your reasons for undertaking

this meditation practice the calming of your mind. It is, however, quite difficult to calm the mind by just using that mind. It can be a bit like trying to pull yourself up by your own bootstraps. Instead, use your body to help calm your mind – if your body is in a good, settled posture, your mind and feelings will follow. To put it another way, if your body slumps, your mind and emotions will too!

Quietly resolve, therefore, to adopt a gentle and reverential attitude towards the meditation practice which follows. Be respectful of the practice, careful in its execution, and unhurried. You should probably spend about twenty minutes on this practice, and do it regularly, though there are no hard and fast rules. The main thing is not to rush.

Once you are settled, inwardly review your actions over the last twenty-four hours. Be aware of those many occasions when you have been helped by others over this period. In what ways have the actions of others supported your existence? For example, silently thank the people who produced, transported and sold your food so that it arrived on your table. You may never meet them, but, however indirectly, they have supported you through their kind actions nonetheless.
Some of these beneficial actions might have been on a large scale, for example, the Love freely given to you by a family member or close friend; others might have been much 'smaller' or more casual, undertaken by perfect strangers; the man who smiled at you as he held a door open for you, or the old lady who wished you a cheery 'good morning' as she passed you in the street. Every little bit helps! While it is undeniable that we have all been the victims of malicious behaviour, of varying degrees of severity and frequency, during our lives, it is salutary to note the positive regard we have been held in by others even over as brief a period as twenty-four hours. Try to be precise and detailed in your recollections.
Then, reflect in a similar manner upon ways in which you, too, have been helpful to others during that same twenty four hour period. This

may be relatively easy to accomplish if you have a job which is somehow bound up with assisting others in some way, and many jobs are.

Even if you haven't got a job like this, you may still be pleasantly surprised to learn how much your existence is helpful to others! You may have offered a word of encouragement, cooked someone a meal, given a loving hug, dried the eyes of a crying child, written 'on the spur of the moment' to someone with whom you had lost touch. If you are in a group whose members have undergone similar experiences, and who offer each other mutual support, remembering how you have helped others may be incredibly easy for you!

Anyway, even a casual audit of your helpful actions will empower you to do even more for others over the NEXT twenty-four hours! Remember that the accumulation of small kindnesses, and their effect in terms of diminishing the world's woes, is as important as the grand charitable gesture!

So, try to think of ways in which you could have done a little more for the welfare of other sentient beings in this 'recent past' that we are contemplating.

Having undertaken the first two parts of this exercise, you may have been left with the impression that what others have done for you outweighs what you have done for others.

If we're honest, perhaps we shouldn't have been short- tempered with that shop assistant, even though he did give us the wrong change. Maybe we could have made the time to chat to the Big Issue seller, instead of scurrying past without buying.

To do this part of the practice is not to wallow in guilt, not to 'beat ourselves up', but simply to recognise that as human beings we are ALL imperfect ( and likely to remain so, however hard we try !) and that a healthy measure of contemplation is the gate through which we pass on the way to making the world a better place.

There are simply no exceptions to this imperfection, however 'religious' a person may be, however, elevated their position in some ecclesiastical hierarchy, whether prince or pauper.

The practice gives us an insight into our shared fallibility as human beings and is enlightening because it puts in the spotlight how we need others and others need us. We grow in wisdom and come to understand what kind of flawed creatures human beings are, ourselves included. Hopefully, we are still sitting in our balanced meditation posture, and have not slumped!

Now let us use our awareness of our imperfection not to make us 'guilty' but to make us kind!

Let us in this final section orientate ourselves towards loving- kindness! What our minds are like is a result of what we think about. If we let our minds dwell upon greed and violence, we will become greedy and violent; if however, we let our minds dwell upon Love, we will become more loving.

So bring to mind loving-kindness, imagine it streaming into your open heart.

If you have a religious faith, or if you have had the benefit of a secure and nurturing background, you may find it relatively easy to locate the source of this Love as somewhere outside yourself.

On the other hand, if you have suffered chronic or acute trauma, it may be that you feel 'blocked off' from such a source, and feel that your capacity to love and be loved has been cruelly and deeply compromised.

This is why the section at the very beginning of this contemplation is so important – it should have made you aware of even the smallest kindnesses performed by others towards yourself and yourself towards others, and show you how you can 'build on' these.

Over the last twenty-four hours, we have all received, at the very least, air to breathe and some food and drink – otherwise we wouldn't still be

alive! The fact that we have survived to the age we are now is testament
to the power of Love!
It may be neither possible nor desirable for you to
ignore the fact that you have experienced truly terrible
things but think on the implications of your survival. You
don't need to worry about whether you can open your heart
to loving-kindness after all you have been through, loving- kindness
itself does the opening for you.
If you are not comfortable with a 'spiritual' vocabulary, that is
absolutely fine – just feel the sun's warmth, take in the oxygen breathed
out by all those green trees, let the rain run down your face. What are
these but the world's Love feeding you and entering the pores of your
skin, making its sure-footed way to your heart
Sit strongly and confidently, visualising this loving-kindness entering
your heart, and infusing your whole being with its warmth.
Remain with this for several minutes. Enjoy the glow. If your mind
wanders, gently bring it back to rest on this sense of Love and goodwill.
Tears may flow – if they do, don't panic! Appreciate the salt taste as
they flow down your cheeks and into your mouth.
You are strong enough because Love is holding you in the palm of its
hand. To keep your resolution firm, you can repeat silently to yourself,
'May all beings be well and happy and safe'.
Once you are confident about letting loving kindness flow into you and
support you, you realise that you don't have to hold onto it, but can let it
go back out again into the world, for the benefit of all suffering beings.
Dedicate the merit of your loving- kindness to all beings everywhere.
Surely, this is what meditation, or contemplation, or prayer, or whatever
you want to call it is – simply allowing Love to flow through you. When
you feel protected by the practice, it is a simple
matter to send your Love back outwards, to
protect others.
Take refuge in your contemplation, and be well and
happy and safe always!

**Pandiculation:** Other animals are very good at this! It is associated with the ability to "re-set" their nervous system to be able to respond to stressful situations. If you have ever watched a cat stretch, they do it from their nose right to the tip of their tail.
We have always been told to "stretch" more, but this is very different from static stretching. This method will re-boot the brain, to relax stiffened muscles and release tension.

When we are talking about this, we use one of my famous "little yellow stretchy men."

1.Stretch the arms of the man outwards as you breathe in, naturally expanding your chest. Then breathe out in your own time, letting the stretchy man's arms return to the normal size. Repeat three times
2.Take the stretchy man's legs, stretch each leg twice,(four stretches in total) as you do this, breathe deeply into the
tummy.Then breathe out as the stretchy man's legs return to the normal size. During this time, you could stretch each of your own legs out and allow them to relax as you breathe out.
3.Hold the stretchy man's shoulders and pull the body down from the man' waist as you take a slow breath in. Breathe out as the stretchy man returns to the normal size. Repeat three times. Obviously, the object of the exercise is not to make the little yellow man stronger, but it is a great way to learn to co-ordinate your breathing and stretching.

Now try and give a BIG yawn! This technique may even trigger a yawn - If it does Go with it! It will help release tension and makes breathing easier. Try this twice a day- or more often if you are tense.
The sense associated with Metal is SMELL.
The sense of smell is unique. Unlike other senses, odour communicates directly to the part of the brain that deals with emotions. Therefore it can produce quick and profound emotional changes.It is thought that human beings are able to smell 1 trillion scents! We have about 400 smell receptors, which isn't as many as other animals, but our more complicated brain compensates for that, meaning we are really good smellers!
We all have our own "Smell World", a little like building up our immune systems for survival, we have similarly built up our repertoire of smells.
So not everyone feels the same way about certain odours.
Our ability to recognise odours does a great deal to shape our mental world. Specific smells can enhance individual emotional states. It made sense when we were evolving to have all of these senses, keeping us safe.
Although we have a personal repertoire, there are a couple of smells that we universally dislike, that smell of vomit and rotten meat. Clearly, they would conjure up thoughts of illness or death!
There is also one smell which we universally like, and that is the smell of rain on the soil or pavement after a dry spell.
It releases chemicals that lift our spirits and is called "Petrichor"
So as soon as you see the rain coming, get out there and smell that magical odour!

I have a particular interest in odours, and am "triggered." by certain ones. I hate the smell of whiskey, stale sweat, and incense; it triggers bad memories of being abused.
I also hate the smell of wallpaper, because when I was being abused, I was scraping the wallpaper off the wall with my fingernails! Of course, I have lots of good smell memories too!
And so have you! It may be a special perfume, or the ocean, flowers, hotdogs, lemons, coffee - whatever.
To further nurture the metal element, I suggest you get (at least) five things that you really like the smell of and make sure they are around you.
We created our "Aromadough" for this purpose, to lift spirits, reduce stress and anxiety.
Our Aromadough is infused with aromatherapy oils blended and designed to calm and soothe the senses while also providing a soft tactile tool that helps you to relax and unwind through the squeezing, rolling action of your hands and fingers.
The brain benefits from two senses being used together, so this fits that bill.
The SMART-UK blend is frankincense, sandalwood and lavender.
It is a calming and uplifting blend designed to meet the needs of our members, their clients and the places where they work.
The blend is also thought to benefit the respiratory problems, abdominal cramps and muscle and joint pains.
In the prison setting, it wasn't possible to have aroma dough; the "putty" is not allowed.
But I was keen to get the same benefits to the prisoners, so much stress reduction needed there.

So I managed to infuse some foam sponge balls with the same organic essential oils, and that magical odour works amazingly well!

The men love them, and they are so popular. Some hang them in their cells; others sleep with them under their pillow! I have been so delighted with the results.

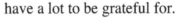

Gratitude needs to be included here, and there's no doubt that many of us in the West have a lot to be grateful for. If you are feeling wretched, it can be a pain when someone says "count your blessings." but it is for your benefit, not to negate the pain you are experiencing.

When I first got into recovery, someone told name if I stayed grateful I would always stay sober! And of course, I am not always grateful, because I am a human being.I have to be reminded!

I suggest that we go to bed with gratitude. Have a notebook at the side of your bed and every night write down at least Five things you are grateful for that day. Sometimes you may be able to fill a book, other times you might be only thankful that you have toilet roll! But if we go to sleep with gratitude, we will sleep better and wake better.

Health     Sobriety

A roof     Music

Food     Dogs

Warmth

Safety    Laughter

Family     Friends

## WATER 水

WATER(In terms of Chinese medicine
the water element is associated
with the Bladder and Kidneys, but that is
not what we are concerned with here.)

The Water element is associated with the winter, a time of conservation
and rest.
If you look out of the window in the winter, you might think that
nothing is happening in nature, the trees are bare, we don't need to cut
the grass, it seems as if everything has died.
But underneath the surface, there is a vast amount going on! All the
growth of the Springtime, blossoming of the Summer, bearing fruit in
Late Summer, and everything that fell in Autumn, is going back into the
Earth to strengthen and conserve energy ready to start the whole cycle
again.
So, although we aren't quite the same as other animals who hibernate in
the winter months, we do need to consider how we can rest and
recuperate!
The Water element is concerned with: **Drive, Determination, Power,
Potential and particularly Brain function.** The emotion associated
with Water is Fear, and the sense associated is Hearing
Everything I have talked about has spotlighted Potential
I have also highlighted the addicts inherent Drive and Determination
Not to mention the whole emphasis on the Brain.
So you can perhaps see that this element is in need of particular care
and attention.

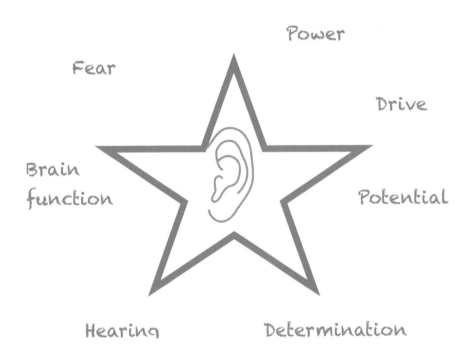

WATER

Power

Fear

Drive

Brain
function

Potential

Hearing

Determination

Water is very Powerful; you only have to watch Water in nature to see how determined it can be! It can drip away and make holes in solid rock, and it can be as powerful as a Tsunami! It can also be tranquil and soothing!

Water is the most Yin function of a human being, therefore if it is deficient, we mean very deficient , so anything that nourishes Yin will help enormously. Remember we are often "creatures of excess".We are very apt to "burn the candle at both ends". We still tend to be "all or nothing", and it is hard for us to to find balance and the middle ground.

Often, as addicts, we have been disempowered, either by the chemicals themselves by the scrapes we find ourselves in, or even by those who think they can help. We have begun to see "powerlessness" as our default position. So time to take back our power and to strengthen this Water element.

RESTORATION is what we are looking for!

In the 24 hours we have in the day and in this ideal world that none of us lives in, we ought to really have 8 hours sleep, 8 hours work, and 8 hours rest and relaxation! I don't know many of us that do that! But trying to be as near to that ideal as we can would be a good idea.

Sleep is so essential for our wellbeing.

These days we moan about not getting enough sleep. But we often ignore the need for darkness.

In ancient times we were not aware of our internal "body clock" or our circadian rhythms, because we didn't have artificial light.Our bodies are still programmed to respond to light and dark as we did then, and it is vital for good health. The sunlight gives us the cue to start our day, the darkness to switch off.

Sleeping in the light disrupts our production of an important hormone "Melatonin" which is crucial for good sleep. At night we "turn off" certain functions like hunger and without that cue from darkness, we disrupt these processes.

We have talked about "empowerment" a lot, so the vital connection with this element is evident.

These rhythms control all living things, and disrupting them are implicated in many health problems, like depression, obesity, even diabetes and breast cancer.

To get a proper nights sleep, we need to cut out any kind of light.

If it is difficult to change curtains or turn off all artificial light, wearing a sleep mask will do the trick! I could not sleep without one!

Don't forget our excellent herbal "Sleep-tea."!

Drinking WATER will help kidney function, when we don't drink enough, we get de-hydrated, and our brains suffer. Drink 1.5 to 2 litres of water a day to keep your brain well hydrated.
Water makes up 83% of the blood, and acts as a transport system, delivering nutrients to the brain, and eliminating toxins. Your brain needs to be fully hydrated so that the circuitry works well.
Water is essential for concentration and mental alertness.
Try drinking your first glass of water when you get up, and then drink the rest of the two liters before lunch time.
Fears can be overwhelming, so it is a good idea to nip them in the bud wherever we can. Have a strategy for when you are panicking or having "flashbacks."
Louise Rooney created this excellent strategy for flashbacks and memories:

Flashbacks and memories can sometimes be powerful, emotional and overwhelming. But they can also be part of the recovery process, and the most important thing to know first is that it is OK that you are having these – it is part of the healing, and you do not need to punish yourself for what happened or the fact that you have these memories.
Firstly take a moment, breath slowly and evenly and remind
Keep breathing – sometimes when we get frightened or anxious and begin to panic, then we don't breathe properly, and that means that we are not getting enough oxygen. This can make panic worse by heightening symptoms such as dizziness, feeling faint, nausea, sweats.
Slowly and evenly breath through the nose and out of the mouth, concentrating only on that breath in and out.
When you feel a little calmer, get in touch with your immediate surroundings – ground yourself in where you are at so that you are clear that you are not back in that dark place. You might stamp your feet or perhaps touch the walls or furniture around you, observing how each thing feels to your touch. Listen to the sounds around you; what can you smell in the air. What are you wearing? How does the fabric feel? What can you see around you?

Often with flashbacks and memories, some people feel like a child again and if this is the case for you then talk to the child in you and remind them that you are OK. Tell the child that it is safe to experience the feelings but that it is not happening again and that you will both work through it together.

Be kind to yourself in a safe way – make sure that you are warm, wrap a blanket around you, hold a pillow or something soft. This is also a great way to make sure that you are aware of where you are.

Get help – this can be a friend or family member who understands about your flashbacks and memories or other useful helplines. You might like to have a plan of action worked out with someone you trust that will mean that you are supported in a way that works for you.

yourself that you are having a flashback and that this is not happening again – the feelings and sensations that you are having are memories about the past.

A plan of action might include soothing music, a gentle phrase that you repeat, having someone be with you or not – your choice – using a familiar thing to hold, watching a favourite movie or programme. If you have a pet, it might be interacting with them, stroking your dog or cat or talking to hamsters etc.

You can take back the control when you are ready – you can remind yourself that the memories are real but that it is not happening again; if this is something that has happened before then you can remind yourself that this will pass, be kind to yourself when you are re-grounded and look after yourself.

When starting to panic  STOP

Think of FIVE things you can see
Four things you can touch
Three things you can hear
Two things you can smell
One thing you can taste

## Use it or Lose it

Learn about the brain! Knowing about it will help you know how to give it the best chance! Your brain is a beautiful, continually developing dense forest with billions of neurons and synapses.

## You are UNIQUE

The brain weighs only 2% of your body mass but takes 20% of the oxygen and nutrients we take. As a general rule you don't need expensive ultra-sophisticated supplements, just learn what's good for you and don't stuff too much "bad stuff" down!

Remember that the brain is part of your body. Things that exercise your body can also help sharpen your mind. Physical exercise enhances neurogenesis.

Look forward to every new day.There's no doubt that "staying in the moment" is a good way of living, but we do need to have something to look forward to, balance once again is key.

Stress and anxiety, no matter where it comes, even your own thoughts, can kill neurons, and prevent the creation of new connections. You can think of chronic stress as the opposite of exercise; it prevents the creation of new synaptic connections.

Learning and mental challenges: The point of having a brain is to learn and adapt to challenging new environments. So challenge your brain often with new activities.

The brain develops no matter what age you are.Try some "Brain training" anything will be helpful, a Crossword a Soduko or any kind of puzzle.

Learn something new every day, it doesn't have to be a huge thing, maybe try and memorise something small, or look something up that you don't already know.

Try a "left-handed day"; if you usually use your Right hand, try swapping it to your left! Eat your dessert before your main course, or, if you typically shower before cleaning your teeth, swap it over! Fool your brain into thinking there is new information coming in. It is all about breaking patterns.

Explore, travel. Adapting to new locations forces you to take more notice of your environment. It may not be possible to travel far, but try being a "tourist" in your own town, see how visitors see it in their eyes! If you can't travel anywhere right now, think about somewhere you would like to visit and learn all about it.

Determination is associated with this element, so even if you have had a bad day, start the next with a determined effort to recover and restore your potential.

Hearing is the sense associated with Water. So think about the sounds you like to hear.It is not surprising to think how important this sense has been in our evolution, so necessary to identify danger signals. There will be sounds for all of us that are mood changing, either good or bad .As with all of these senses, each sound will have different connotations.

Pick at least FIVE sounds that lift your spirits; It might be music or the sound of the ocean; the sound of drumming or tapping, a choir or rustling leaves, some individual voices make you feel better, listen to them often, record them if you can.

Some voices you might hate the sound of, and once again can be "triggers" avoid them wherever you can! Put sounds that make you feel good on your phones or a player of some kind. Remember these senses have been honed for our survival, so don't underestimate them!

One of the most healing sounds is of a cat purring! Cats purr at a particular frequency, exactly 26 Hertz. This frequency corresponds with the frequency that scientists use in vibrational therapies to promote tissue regeneration. But it is not only for healing tissues; it is also beneficial for reducing stress and anxiety levels! So if you have a cat - great! If not, record the sound of one purring and use it as part of your armour.

Animals of all kinds are therapeutic, if you stroke a dog you get a shot of the "cuddle" hormone Oxytocin, the dog gets it too! So it is a reciprocal treatment! if you don't have a dog, stroke someone else's!

MUSIC has been known to be therapeutic for centuries!you can see how much it affects us by the goosebumps we get when we hear a particular piece of music, even if we don't know the words!

We are a pattern seeking species and music is all about patterns! We tend to gravitate to other people with our own musical tastes, jazz fans with jazz fans, opera fans with the same.It is valuable social cohesion!

Singing is especially beneficial, it increases endorphins, improves lung function, increases oxygen to the brain,. I sing in my car on long journeys!! But like everything we have talked bout, the benefits are doubled when we do things with others! So try a choir, it doesn't have to be a church choir, there are many wonderful secular choirs around these days.

Be a good listener. Ears don't get us into trouble like our mouths often do! Learn conscious, active listening, it improves your brain and nurtures that Water element.

Try "journaling." It will help you discover things about you.
Journaling isn't the same as keeping a diary that logs the things you do
or see – it is a way of expressing your thoughts, clarifying your feelings
and trying to find a sense of self, an exploration of
who you are, where you have been, and the person you would like to
become.
It's a useful way of putting some order into your thoughts, perhaps
helping to solve immediate problems that come up, it's a way of putting
it into a format that you can readily see. It's often used as a way of
working through trauma, helping to release some of the feelings, fears
and thoughts that surround the events.
I have created this "5 Star wellbeing journal." for just this purpose!
But of course, you can use any that you prefer.

You may have mountains to climb, but having enough "fuel" and a plan
to keep refilling it as a way of life will empower you and make all
things more possible.
Aim for optimum brain health. So along with a brain strengthening diet,
meditation, exercise, sleep, try the following numbers daily.

I love numbers, they have often helped me make sense of things around me.

So take good care of those FIVES! Gather them around you and keep them close:

FIVE things to look at.

FIVE tastes.

FIVE things you like to touch.

FIVE smells.

FIVE sounds,

FIVE champions: They are your "Dream team"!

Here is another sequence to remember! A good plan for every day.

## 2-5-8-10-20-30

2 litres of water

5 pieces of fruit and veg a day

8 hours of sleep

10 minutes of meditation

20 minutes of exercise

30 minutes to eat your meals.

Try and stay in the moment. A day at a time is good advice. Anyone can cope with anything for 24 hours that would be unthinkable if they had to do it forever.

Remember the word

H.A.L.T.

It stands for Hungry, Angry, Lonely, Tired.

If you are feeling "out of sorts, It may be because of any of these, so before you reach for the nearest drink or pill, ask yourself "Am I Hungry?" so eat something, "Am I angry?" deal with it, "Am I lonely?" Speak to someone, "Am I Tired?" get some rest!

## Chapter Nine
### The Smart-UK Community

It would be impossible to put into words how privileged I feel to have taught so many wonderful people. Every year I meet up with them all again, ostensibly for their supervisions, but secretly so I get to see them all again and have hundreds of hugs!

The song says"If you become a teacher, by your students you'll be taught" and it is so true, they have taught me so much I could not have wished for a better professional experience than I have had with these and so many others I have taught.

A few of them wanted to add their voice to this story, and it is very humbling to say the least!

## Rachel Palethorpe manager HMPS.

Meeting Sue and the course changed my perspectives on addictions completely'

Working with addictions can be difficult and frustrating, and when I have days when I feel that way,I think about things I learned on the SMart-UK course and it refills my empathy and patience.

The sentence "We are all made of stardust" is something I still tell patients (and friends and family) when they are struggling: Thirteen years after first discovering Sue and auricular acupuncture.

Understanding, not only how our brains work, but also to see the potential in everyone made finding empathy for everyone not only essential, but easier to do.

Auricular Acupuncture became and still remains an essential part of service delivery in every service I have managed, because of it's amazing impact and outcomes.

I often recall a personal story Sue shared with us on the course about her own life and how our brains react to danger.Being able to help people understand why thy are feeling how they feel is so empowering! That's a gift from Sue that I have been able to share with others.

Sue has been a massive inspiration to me, meeting her and attending that training course all those years ago undoubtedly made me start to look for the potential in everyone, and now, when I meet addicts in the grips of their addiction, I imagine a beautiful garden of flowers they are going to be, not just the work in progress they are at the time.

Sue has an endless amount of enthusiasm and kindness and it is so contagious! I have worked with so many colleagues over the years who have gone on to complete training with Sue, and every single one comes away revitalized and excited.

In times where services are being defunded, and addicts continue to be stigmatized, Sue and her expertise, kindness is needed more than ever in this sector.

Who would have thought you would have prisoners,(not always the best behaved) in a high security prison, all asking for acupuncture sessions!It's popularity spoke for itself.

## Billy Little NHS

I've been lucky enough to be part of this inspirational treatment provided by Smart-UK in HM Prisons and Sue Cox is still contributing and dedicating her life to making a difference.

I owe my passion for Auricular Acupuncture to Sue and her team, who still continue to be enthusiastic and motivated to change .I have great admiration for Smart-UK , continue to excel and continue to be the front runners in the use of Auricular Acupuncture in Substance misuse treatment.

Billy Little ( ex -Prison officer DSPD unit HM Prison Frankland )

PAUL REYNOLDS NHS Hartlepool

I first met with Sue after enrolling onto SMART UK Auricular Acupuncture training in 2017. I had heard some amazing stories from colleagues about Sue's training and had seen the fantastic results of Auricular Acupuncture with clients I was working with. I asked my then line manager in HMP Holme House, when I worked for Lifeline if I could enrol onto the training. To my delight this was agreed.

I completed the 4 day training programme with Sue along with colleagues from across the prison establishments in the North East of England. I have got to say that from walking into the training room and meeting the warm, smiling face of Sue I felt at ease straight away, although a little nervous about putting needles into peoples ears.

Sue's training was fantastic from start to finish. Sue's wealth of knowledge, passion and commitment shines through in every sentence she delivers from explaining how we are all made of

I left the Prison establishment for my own professional development and now work in local authority working with individuals who suffer from addiction. Auricular Acupuncture was not a treatment on offer when I first started and I advocated Sue's training to management who could clearly identify the benefits of this treatment.

I personally ran 4 sessions of Auricular Acupuncture weekly, one of which was on an evening to accommodate individuals work needs. The sessions became more popular and a need was identified to have other members of staff trained, which is what happened so we could add extra sessions to the timetable.

Sue has always said "Give me a ring if you need any advice" I have asked Sue's advice on other aspects of my professional decision making and Sue's advice has always supported me in making the right decisions for me.

I have recently acquired Sue's 5 star well-being journal and use this not only for myself but the content is so useful for every ones well-being. I am hopeful that we can work with Sue for future training and I feel that when you have been trained from Sue you feel like you a part of a VERY LARGE family sharing the knowledge gained from Sue with others we support

This training has been the best training I have ever completed since I started working in addiction and recovery.

**Kay W-D** psychologist HMP. Frankland

'One of Sue's strengths is that she always works with alignment to her values. There is always a sense of genuine care for the person (whether that be a service user, a member of staff, or someone else), the drive to go beyond what is expected in order to connect with a person. She has a strengths-based and holistic approach, which is inspiring'. §

There are so many more of these wonderful people, I am grateful to every one of them As are the really rather famous people who have sent messages of encouragement! See the page on our website

https://smart-uk.com/about-us/messages-of-encouragement/

## Chapter Ten
### HM Prison  Holme House

I have talked a lot about my pride in the partnership I have with Her Majesty's prison service. It remains one of my greatest privileges.

Everyone I have ever taught is terrific, prison staff are especially deserving of mention, they work in such difficult circumstances and are rarely honoured.

I must though, single out HMP Holme House, a prison in Stockton on TeesI that I have taught in for many years.

It is here that the latest Smart-UK evolution has taken place, where the next part of our extended family the "5-star Wellbeing coaches" are based.

A conversation began when one particular prison asked me if it might be possible to teach some prisoners to administer Acupuncture on each other.

The idea in itself was well-intentioned, but for a variety of reasons I didn't think it appropriate.To facilitate a training course of that nature would have been fraught with obstacles, not least obtaining insurance.!

But after that conversation, and an idea began to germinate.

I had always thought it would be most rewarding for me to be able to go direct to the "patient group" themselves, to teach them what the workers learn.

I am a great believer in "owning" our recoveries, of becoming empowered, not further disenfranchised. I think if anyone has any difficulty, then full knowledge of their situation is crucial if they want to make a lasting change.

So when I then was asked to teach an overview of the theories to some of those men, I was delighted, and that began a fantastic process that has seen them soar.

They have become enabled to use their existing compassion for their peers and add some valuable practical skills to be tremendous supports and influencers. I have been blown away by their dedication and willingness to embrace new concepts and utilize them for the good of others.

They learn everything that the staff know, apart from actually using needles. They understand the Chinese theories, and how they translate in the West, they learn about the brain and its importance and how they can help each other achieve optimum brain health.

They learn acupressure other natural interventions, and how they can help with anxiety, depression, poor sleep patterns as well as addiction issues. They are a veritable army of help! I am so proud of them!!!

Of necessity, prisons are utilitarian, and there is very little of a "poetic" or "beautiful" nature inside them! Yet, research shows how human beings definitely respond to authentic kindness.

This is not a "fluffy" approach, and I am aware that there have been serious crimes committed, and by extension, damaged victims. But no one is served by not allowing people to see the possibilities of change and restoration.

I wanted them to discover  the fantastic survival skills they have and how they can reconnect with them, learn a few more,  and use them to gain their true potential.

Prisoners actually have amazingly honed skills; they have had to navigate a host of obstacles, abusive, violent situations to name but a few.

For example, research has shown that as human beings we are adept at telling "lies": exaggerating our achievements, wearing makeup, puffing ourselves up to find a mate, get that career, in fact, survive! Other animals do it too, look at their elaborate mating rituals, peacocks tail feathers, toads puffing up their throats, making themselves look the biggest, most impressive, more "mate-worthy" even playing dead!

What the research also says is that we aren't that great at spotting lies in others! The worst at lie-spotting among us are the most unlikely: police, doctors, lawyers! The very BEST at it are prisoners!! Of course they are! they have had to be! When I told some of our prisoners about this research, it came as no surprise to them at all!

I was thrilled at how much they took to this programme and embraced these new concepts. What had started as a two-day workshop, became much more, we created and trained 17 prisoners to become "5 Star wellbeing coaches", and they are active and thriving in HMP Holme House.

smart<sub>UK</sub>

# Wellbeing Coach

Their role is to pass on information and self-help tools to their peers.They are able to use acupressure to help with a variety of difficulties.They have a case full of "props" that they can use to make a real difference.

It has been exciting and unbelievable to see the melding of the utilitarian prison system and the "touchy-feely" acupuncture world! They learn all of the theories taught to the staff, apart from putting in needles. I am now rolling that out to other establishments, and organisations, and as always, I am also learning from them all the time.

I believe this programme can be used anywhere by anybody

I had always thought it would be most rewarding for me to be able to go direct to the "patient group" themselves, to teach them what the workers learn.

I am a great believer in "owning" our recoveries, of becoming empowered, not further disenfranchised. I think if anyone has any difficulty, then full knowledge of their situation is crucial if they want to make a lasting change.

So when I then was asked to teach this overview of the theories to some of those men, I was delighted, and that began a fantastic process that has seen them soar.

They have become enabled to use their existing compassion for their peers and add some valuable practical skills to be tremendous supports and influencers. I have been blown away by their dedication and willingness to embrace new concepts and utilize them for the good of others.

They learn acupressure other natural interventions, and how they can help with anxiety, depression, poor sleep patterns as well as addiction issues. They are a veritable army of help! I am so proud of them!!! I feel a great affinity with those in prison.

Of course, I could not do these things without the support of the prison and some fantastic colleagues, Mike Wheatley, the two Rachels and the excellent Sammy Wilson.

They deserve to tell this themselves!

**Sammy Wilson** Community Co-ordinator HMPrison Holme House.

The 5 Star Well-being Programme

Working within the field of substance misuse I have often found myself feeling frustrated with the idea of us promoting a service that is 'lead by the service user' when in actual fact the service user has had very little, to no input into the services delivered. This is where my passion for lived experience and service user voice was born. I wanted to make a difference by promoting the importance of lived experience and its power.

We must remember that the people accessing our services are not stupid; these people are intelligent, hardworking, dedicated and strong. They have faced some of the most difficult situations and seen some of the most horrific things, yet they are still able to see the light.

I was delighted when I was given to opportunity to support Sue in the delivery of her Acupressure training back in 2018 for recovery month. This was the first time this training would be delivered to a group of prisoners. I had heard so much about Sue from colleagues.

The training went down really well with the Men, they engaged fully and were taught an awful lot within those two days, but not only that, Sue empowered them to start taking ownership of their own recovery by understanding how the brain works, why certain behaviours occur and most importantly what they could do about it without relying on anyone else.

When the training came to an end, the men said they didn't want this to be the end, and they wanted to do something more with this, and share the knowledge they had far a wide amongst their community to help others feel empowered the way they did.

This was where The 5 Star wellbeing coach scheme was born. The men were involved from the offset and have shaped the scheme to be what they want.

Two years later, we have a team of 14 Coaches who can offer advice and support to their peers, sharing knowledge and helping people to feel better. They have been able to showcase their work during visits from NHS England and MOJ who have been blown away by their involvement and dedication to the programme.

It makes me really proud to see how passionate the men are about the scheme and I can say I truly believe the service users are at the heart of everything SMART UK and The 5 Star coach scheme deliver.

Sue, along with the men in HMP Holme House, has created a positive community, empowering and enabling men to reach their

potential.
As for me, I see myself on a journey which so far has taken me exactly where I wanted to go within my career. A journey that has allowed me to explore more about lived experience and its value. I will continue to promote this and create opportunities which will enable people to grow. Thank you, Sue, for working alongside us in HMP Holme House and making all of this amazing work possible! We are forever grateful for everything you do and look forward to where ever this journey takes us next.

And from some of the men:
**Chris F.resident HMP Holme House**
I am Chris, and I am a 5-star wellbeing coach. I believe that it has made a real difference to the men and me in HMP Holme House.I am a veteran of the British army and suffer from Post- traumatic stress disorder. Becoming a five-star wellbeing coach has given me a lot of pride and helped with my confidence and the ability to deal with life's struggle.

In the past, I didn't have any alternatives. I can now use different techniques and share those with the men and other veterans who also have Post Traumatic stress disorder. They maybe have anxiety, they can't sleep because of flashbacks which are part of their PTSD. Before coming to Holme House I was constantly making the same mistakes over and over again. Problems lead to alcohol, lead to drugs, lead to even more problems. This was a cycle that was never ending. Not dealing with my emotions, problems, relationship, fatherhood and responsibilities. Living in abusive households throughout my childhood witnessing DV, drug addiction, violence towards myself left me very vulnerable as a child and growing up as a young adult.
Leading into my mistake which is why I am in Holme House. I suffered a series of mental health breakdowns and spend a short period of time in a mental hospital.
Coming to jail , leaving my two children and family, stepping away from my toxic unhealthy lifestyle was, looking now, a life saver and

given me opportunities to become now more equipt and build more resilience for the future.

Being abstinent and engaging with DART, Mental health and working on lots of positive projects within Holme House, I was placed onto the 5 star wellbeing coach training thanks to Sammy, Rachael Moore and Sue Cox.

The training was over 2 days and was very detailed and educational. I learnt so much. A lot of what Sue was teaching us was really making so much sense to me and making me think

Having never really made serious life mess ups without being full of Alcohol or drugs seeing, understanding how my brain works was making a lot of sense and making me more focused and switched on.

This was all giving me a lot of excitement, enthusiasm and drive to stay in control, use my experiences in a positive way and remain sober myself and mentally, emotionally more tooled up for a healthy future.

I spent many years not caring about myself or how my brain works, to now gaining a better understanding and caring was so empowering.

Becoming a 5 star wellbeing coach with the skills, the case, the pride which all came with it was amazing. The fact I could and have so many times give men acupressure to help men with anxiety, sleep as well as having wellbeing days for staff and men to promote what we do.

Helping so many different people, in so many individual ways, making such a difference to the men's daily life is what makes the training so valuable.

I was able to incorporate the skills I learnt in my role as Gym Orderly and Veteran lead offering Acupressure in the Health and wellbeing gym session and VIC's meetings supporting fellow PTSD sufferers and help support and encourage positive lifestyle choices to all men and staff.

about my past in much more detail and with more emotional attachment and realisation. Helping me relate to my past behaviour, thoughts and feelings.

To be able to make such a difference with our role and help so many gives me so much pride and motivation to keep helping more people.

Thank you Sue Cox for making such a difference, empowering so many and making us smile.

Making a difference together.


**Steven Resident HMP Holme House**
Wellbeing and me
Hello,
My name is Steven, and I am an alcoholic, the reason I can say that now is because I now have the gift that is recovery, I needed recovery because my addiction had taken me to rock bottom.
I was charged with attempted murder and sentenced to 15 years. I was sent to HMP Durham, and it was at this point I asked myself how and why this has happened? See after five years of being sober. I now realize my recovery and wellbeing journey started with one word; that word is yes!
My addiction has beaten me into submission; I was sick of being sick. I realized I had the gift of desperation, desperate not to let this happen again, so when asked if I wanted help the word out of my mouth was yes, when any other time I would have said no.
Once I received my recovery, which is a whole life change, I because open-minded to the holistic approach, every part of my life needed to change. I came to HMP Holme House where I applied for a service user rep job as I had been engaged with DART for four years at this point, this is how I met Sammy, she gave me the job.
It wasn't long after that she mentioned about becoming a Wellbeing coach. I had used Acupuncture and found it benefitted me, and I would meditate while having the needles in I found it helped me deal with the pressures of prison life, so when asked I said yes. I was told it was a two-day course, and instead of needles, we would use seeds, but the principles were the same as Acupuncture.
This is how I met Sue Cox; she had a passion for wellbeing as I did for recovery. We were taught the history of Acupuncture, how it works and how to do it for others. We also look at diet; I was introduced to herbal tea which I found relaxing. I think it would benefit other prisoners too.

As a wellbeing coach, when we get the opportunity, we can apply seeds to other prisoners to help them with anxiety, headaches and nausea. Above all though being a wellbeing coach is about using my own experience to help others. I would like to thank Sammy for putting me on the course and the support she has given me to get me where I want to be, to Sue who has taught me that when you are passionate about what you do, it is not a job, it is a vocation. I will be forever grateful, and as I am sober, I will never forget. And to the still suffering addicts, hold on, pain ends, it works if you work it.

Thanks,

Steven

### Dion L: resident HMP Holme House

The first time I was a prisoner, I was thirteen years old. I have been a prisoner for the past thirty years.

This is the first programme or course, or even the first bit of learning that actually empowers us to help ourselves on our own level. Not repeating mantras- that doesn't help—someone else's words.

Sue does not do "dumbed down". We are taught all the science and about the brain. We get all aspects of the wellbeing, all about sleep, food, stillness and empowerment. I think it shows people how to balance themselves. You aren't always having to go to someone else and then someone else, being more dependent.

Obviously, we have lost our freedom, but prison can be really emasculating, and often some of the things we get infantilize us, treat us like children you know. Something like this is empowering, like REALLY empowering , not only to get through the current problems but for life in real general growth and all that.

### David B- resident, HMP Holme House

My name is David, and I am a resident here in HMP Holme House. I am also, and thankfully a 5-star wellbeing coach, I feel really proud of this, It is something totally different here I do a lot of interventions on the wing I am resident on.

We have a lot of guys that have had issues with substance misuse, addiction. We have an age range from younger guys to older guys who have suffered of with a lot of trauma in their lives.
We work with a range of guys; the feedback I get is amazing. Maybe someone in the first stages of triggers and cravings, or
perhaps someone has had a bad phone call from his girlfriend. It is all across the board, and it has really helped me personally, in fact, I think it has made me the man I am today.
When I am released, I want to take this forward and help in the community; it has been life-changing.

Jamie resident HMP Holme House

I am. Jamie and I am on House block six, which is the therapeutic wing. I have found being a "5-star coach" very helpful for myself and the other lads. Especially over Christmas time and January, people missing their families, wanted help with sleep, relaxation. It has been good for all of us that have taken part in this.

Tyrone resident HMP Holme House
I am Tyrone from house block 2, and I am a 5-star mentor coach for Sue Cox. It makes me happy to know I can help others that I am not the only one with problems, and I can give back. I do lots of stuff for the lads, for lots of reasons, they all benefit. It is great stuff!

Ryan resident HMP Holme House
I am Ryan, and I am a 5-star coach on House block one. I have been helping the guys in difficulty, especially over the Christmas time, I give them acupressure and stuff, and if I a called out, I go on all the spurs on the wing to see them. It is such good stuff.

**DION L resident HMP Holme House**

I am the Young person's mentor in HMP Holme House, and I have been for a couple of years. From all my experiences in the prison system and mentoring different groups.,

I noticed that the hardest group to reach are the "Y.O's" the under twenty fours. They don't access any services, maybe because they haven't hit a wall yet, come to the realization that they have issues or problems.

They still feel indestructible. But they do have issues, and they build up in them, and the problems have snowballed. They have gained some bad habits and made terrible life choices. All that learned behaviour. They won't get a health screening, or access drug and alcohol services; they try and cope on their own in the wings. Last year when we did the Young person's group, we gave them a taster of the 5-star wellbeing programme. They took to Sue, and they took to Sue's programme amazingly, thirty young lions all in a room together, and not average people either! A couple of them have even gone on to become coaches. This is a good thing because this might be the first positive step that some of them have ever made in their lives. Sue is inspiring, not just her story and knowledge but her character, she is a really genuine character, and we know that we know when someone is real. I think she deserves her props and respect.

Thank you to all of the men who are taking part in this, and all those yet to come! You have inspired me, humbled me and made me proud. I now am rolling this out to other establishments, But you will ALWAYS be the pioneers and close to my heart!

## ChapterEleven

### Superheroes

---

Now I want you to hear from some of my favourite **"Superheroes"**, who have been to Hell and are quietly going about using their "Superpowers" to inspire! In fact simply seeing their names written here makes me smile and fills me with pride and admiration.

## Dayamay Dunsby:

There Has to Be a Substitute.

The story of my journey is not that different to most of the other unfortunate people who's lives have been devastated by addiction, social dysfunction and mental illness.

The thing that makes mine an exceptional story is the fact that I, by some miracle, lived to tell the tale with my sanity reasonably in-tact. This is in no small part thanks to my long-term friend (arguably my first ever real friend therapist (acupuncture) and source of inspiration Sue Cox. She was there for me and managed to reach my broken heart when the rest of the world had written me off. For this I am eternally indebted and greatly humbled.

I grew up in an alcoholic, socially dysfunctional hell hole in the midlands, England. My mother had lost her first child some five years before I was born and was addicted to prescription drugs, namely valium, the 'wonder drug' of the time, before anyone had detected the chronic side effects which included severe addiction. Mixed with the alcohol that she drank every day in a frantic and desperate fashion, this became the solution to her personal hell and came at the ultimate price of her sanity.

She was and still is a shell of a person. My father was a 'functional' alcoholic who hid behind his ability to go out into the world and provide for the family. This was part and parcel of his addictive complex, and the hard worker image suited his agenda well because he didn't have to face the responsibility of his home life, which was deteriorating all the time. Any spare time that he got was spent holed up in the kitchen, swilling cider and strong lager and rowing constantly with my deranged mother!

There were regular violent occurrences, sometimes involving us but usually between them as they thrashed out their pain on each other, repeating the same tired themes over and over again like some recurring nightmare. My first memory was of my mother producing a carving knife from under her pillow and attempting to stab my Dad, who had his back to her and was only alerted to the danger because I had called out in terror.

I now know that the reason that this holds such a prominent place in the archives of my mind is because it was etched in by the sheer trauma of the event!

The job of the parents is to provide safe conditions for their children to grow in and to teach them how to negotiate and function in the world with all its pitfalls. What I learned from my parents was to be scared, and that alcohol and other substances were the answer to everything.

This example became the basis for my default setting, to escape the pain by whatever means and deal with the consequences with more of the same. It worked pretty well for some time, depending on who's perspective you were looking from.

By the time I was sixteen I was riddled with addiction! I didn't know it but every thought that I had was centred around the avoidance of my pain and the pursuit of pleasure. I hid behind the bravado of the drug culture which seemed to conceal my inadequacy in some areas but would regularly fail in one way or another, leaving me exposed, desperate and vulnerable.

By the time I reached my late teens I was so full of pain that it was bursting through the façade no matter how much I drank or used. I had learned to hide my emotions because they were dangerous and often led to more of the pain that I was trying so desperately to avoid.

At this point though my anger and frustration were impossible to contain as the conditions in my life, particularly at home, became impossible. I didn't realise that I was being constantly triggered by my family, who represented a constant rejection and abandonment trauma!

It all became too much and I lost control of my anger, causing my parents to kick me out. I had just turned 18 but was as helpless as a child and psychologically little more!

This was the point of real crisis where the problems escalated, drug and alcohol use increased, both in the potency of the substances and the frequency with which I used them.

I hit bottom and my spirit broke. Physically and mentally I fell apart and I eventually sought the ultimate escape by trying to take my own life! This made things even worse. I no longer knew if people really liked me or just felt sorry for me as a suicide case! This was excruciating.

The power of addiction is such that my misery and suffering continued pretty much as it had been for another 15 years, despite the frantic efforts of many people, professional and otherwise, to help me find some sort of peace. I heard sanity but couldn't quite connect with it.

People like Sue Cox spent many hours trying to provide me with something that would inspire me into recovery. A part of me knew that this was the only way for me and I started to fight for my life by accepting the help that was offered to me. It was not easy and took several years before it really seemed as if I was getting anywhere.

I ended up in a treatment centre which seemed to have the level of care available for what I needed. When the drugs and alcohol came away all of my physical and psychological symptoms came to the surface and life became very difficult.

The withdrawal process was long and painful and the first stage went on for many weeks. Luckily I recognised that, painful as it was, this was an opportunity to change the story and so I stuck around and tried to make a go of it. At this time I re- discovered 12 step fellowships which were a great inspiration and provided the perfect springboard for total abstinence and permanent recovery.

As my head began to clear I started to reflect on the teachings that I had received from Sue. She had been very passionate and that passion had made an impression that stays with me to this day. Sue had armed me with enough information about the neurological processes of addiction that I knew not to take the problem too lightly or myself too seriously.

Complacency can kill in recovery just as quickly as ego or self-pity! She had helped me to see that the very characteristics which define the chronic addict are actually, at a biological level, remnants of extraordinary ability and capacity for achievement which set us aside from the average Human in prehistoric times.

Our propensity for excess is a function of an innate survival drive which probably enabled us to be more successful hunter gatherers and providers for our families.

With modern societies achievements in technology and the advancing of social conditions, there is no longer a need or a place for this behaviour, but our brains still produce the necessary output for the role. We are biologically wired for a higher level of performance which has been rendered redundant.

Addiction is the modern equivalent and manifestation of this neurological anomaly; the brain attempting to fulfil impulses that no longer have a social or practical application in our abundant lives.

With the drugs and alcohol removed we are delivered back to the same dilemma. Overactive brain function and insufficient stimulation and fulfillment! There has to be a substitute! This was a tough lesson for me and one that, when I eventually heeded it, formed the basis for the rebuilding of my life in a much more productive and positive direction. Creativity replaced dependency and destructive behaviours as I began to channel this special aptitude toward recovery.

I am now a socially engaged, ordained Buddhist monk, with a lot of hobbies. Meditation is a tool that has proved invaluable for coping with the seemingly random surges of brain activity that occur frequently.

Meditation strengthens the part of the brain that can override excessive brain activity when it is not appropriate, like a reconditioning process. I have been meditating for a good few years and feel like it plays an important part in the long-term healing of my body and mind after many years of severe abuse.

Recovery is a true blessing, a highly interesting and pleasurable journey with benefits that reach well beyond my own personal experience, producing positive ripples that help to create the conditions of hope for many more to come.

Dayamay

## Kevin Neary: Aid And Abet Edinburgh

Kevin Neary My Purpose

I was born into a family of 6 older siblings, living in a one-bedroom living room kitchen known then as a "Single-end "in the east end of Glasgow. The pressure was already on, and I hadn't even opened my eyes yet.

The only sense that I had was of my hearing at a tender age of four days old, and this is what was going to condition me from this day forward. What I hear and see will condition me for my future outcome, and I don't even know it.

Four years old we move to a three-bedroom in another part of Glasgow known as the "Wine ally," I watch a knife fight between my father and two other men, horrific scenes for a four- year-old to watch and witness. No one comes to young Kevin and says "how did that experience make you feel"?" how do you feel now wee man" can you describe those emotions!

No one ever asked me how I felt! Going to school at five FEAR penetrated me every day, and I didn't know it. At that age, I thought this was normal but very uncomfortable, and I hated how I felt.

Going to school with bust shoes, socks sticking through the holes in my shoes in the pouring rain. But school was my safe place, and I loved my wee school in Glasgow. One of the teachers took me out the class one day and took me in her car, bought me new shoes, new socks, and sent me home with a letter to say to my parents that they hoped my parents would not be offended that they realised we did not have much.

Going home from school was when I was most at fear; going home to alcoholism, verbal shouting swearing, and domestic abuse. I found I had no appetite to eat and just wanted to run away. What I was hearing and seeing was affecting me and my future, and I don't even know it.

We move away from Glasgow, yet no one informs me we are moving, no one tells me I won't be going back to my school where I felt safe and wanted. I'm taken to a new school, a new community of people and I'm terrified. I don't like where I live, and I don't like the teachers, the school, or the people in it, in fact, I don't like me!!

I sit in class I can't concentrate my hands' sweat, my stomach churns round and round, waiting on the dreadful bell to ring, like a boxer that goes out for the tenth round, as I'm scared to go home to the drinking and violence that happens most weekends.

I'm terrified on a Sunday night because I'm riddled with fear, I hate school and don't want to be there. I'm in constant flight or fight mode, and again, I don't know it because at this time in my life no one ever asks wee Kev "How are you feeling wee man? "

Many times I run away from school, many times I'm removed from the class. This continues into my secondary school where I'm now being conditioned with a belief system that no one cares, and I have to fight everything and everybody to keep safe. I'm in constant turmoil I'm being ripped apart from the inside out with Fear anxiety worry. I have no purpose in life; I have no direction.

Aged 13 one November night I pick up a bottle of strong wine with a friend and drink it. Instant effect! Fear, worry, anxiety are removed from me from that second. I have found a solution to all this internal turmoil, and I feel beautiful, I feel free for the first time in many years, I'm at one with me.

I'm a milk boy earning money to get to the weekend to buy my drink and get respite from my previous days. What I don't know is that when I'm drinking, all this buried emotion and anger resentment, to everyone is going to come out like a tsunami and anyone or anything in my way is going to be on the receiving end of verbal and physical abuse.

This resulted in me being excluded from school, being excluded was part of my conditioning, as I never felt included and always excluded from everything. I even wondered if I was adopted? I never felt included in my family, where by this stage, I had Five brothers three sisters who all cared about me, but I couldn't see it.

By the age of 17 years, I'm now in the criminal justice system doing my first stint of many in a young offender's institution. While I'm in there, I'm back to being full of fear anxiety. I promise myself I won't drink, I don't want to go back to prison.

The drinking escalates, the crimes get bigger; my journey into adult prison becomes longer stays. My progression goes into drug addiction; smoking weed popping prescription drugs. Not any particular prescription drug, but anything that said on the packet "Do not drive or operate machinery. May cause drowsiness: I eat them!! This led on too many years of cocaine and Heroin addiction 20+ years and all the behaviours and choices which became no choice that comes with the lifestyle, and I have no purpose or direction.

Mid 2006, my house is surrounded by armed police. They have come for a gunfight as I've committed a crime with a gun. At this point, I have lost every relationship. Mother, Father, brothers, sisters, son, intimate personal, working relationships are gone. I have nothing to live for. I'm like a shattered widescreen on the insides. My thinking is saying to me "I'll just get them to end it!

Through the professionalism of a police negotiator on the phone, they managed to talk me out my thinking, and away from another idea of my delusional thinking.
Following their specific, clear cut instructions, I left the house. Hands behind my head, one step at a time, an audience of neighbours, police cars, and police marksmen.    "One step at a time" the voice is shouting.

"Stop! Drop to one knee" I look down to the ground as I go down to kneel, and there I see Red dot's floating around my chest, at this point on seeing the red dots knowing how serious this is, I don't want to die! I don't want to die!

This takes me into a long term prison sentence, back in the system, receiving 120 mls of methadone daily to maintain me through the day. A methadone program that I had been on for ten years. A program has a start and finish to it, but this program never had an end. I always wondered why they called it a program!

Six months into the sentence, I don't engage, I hate authority, I hate everyone. I'm doing it Kev's way, not realising Kev's way has never worked - how could it work with no direction or purpose in life. One day a prison staff member comes asked me if I intend on moving on through the system and getting my parole.

How? Why? Move on to what,? I'm struggling to understand about getting out. I don't want out -I have nothing to go out to! Why would I want out? And if I did, what would I have to do? The staff member offers me C.B.T (cognitive behavioural therapy) and ( self-management and recovery training) Alcohol awareness, drug awareness.

Then proceeds to say how I need to change the way I think feel and behave, about my actions, choices, consequences, empathy. On and on he goes "Stop! I say" "You want me to rewire my thinking, thoughts? Feelings? Behaviours? Change everything about me so I can get out of prison? I have nothing to go out to"! No family, friends, son. I don't get visits; I don't write letters, I don't receive letters, I don't do phone calls. "You want me to change ?

It's too late! I have nothing, why change or even consider change at this point in my life"? This stuff you're offering should have been given to me at ten years old, not when I'm 30+ when I'm broken busted, disgusted, and cannot be trusted!" Mentally, physically emotionally and spiritually bankrupt with no purpose or direction.

"This stuff your offering should be taken into schools and given to kids at ten, not when it's too late. Early intervention and prevention, that's what should have happened to me, maybe I wouldn't be here in this institution or this situation with life right now".

At this point, I say to the staff member "This should be taken into schools - and I should be taking it into schools! Talking about the consequences of your actions, empathy, feelings, thoughts, behaviour's choices, and talking about what happened in my life, and maybe they won't have to live my past"!

The staff member said. "What makes you think you taking this stuff into school would work?" I then tell him the Snowball story. You see when I was in the second year at school., the school brought in a blind man with his guide dog to collect money that was being raised for the blind. During his visit, kids asked him questions. "What's your dog's name?" What does your dog do for you?" "What time is it? "A kid asked, the man feels around his watch," half-past two" the man reply's everyone applauded. "Do you dream?" a kid asks? "Yes, I dream - people born blind don't get visual when they dream they get sound and smell or shadow, but I get visual because I could see until I was twelve years old it's the only time I see is when I dream." Another kid asks "how did you go blind"? "I got hit in the head with a Snowball, it had a stone in it, and was knocked unconscious, and I never saw again.

I stopped flinging snowballs even to this day every time I see someone flinging snowballs I think of that blind man. "Suppose I could go into schools and talk about feelings, thoughts, behaviours, empathy, choices.

And what happened in my life. It's not just a snowball we are talking about -its life or death! And that's why I think I could take this into schools".

The staff member comes back with "You will never work in schools, big man, you're a junkie! Heroin addict alcoholic committed many crimes on a very high dose of methadone, and if you are considered for early release you have a three-year extension on your license, I think it best you get that right out your head and think about getting out early.

I went to my prison cell and reflected on my life at this point. I dropped to my knees and cried & cried and sobbed like a baby. Not because of what the staff member said, but because for the first time in my life, I found out I had a purpose. As I reflected and realised that there are so many kids out there without direction, purpose, no dreams or vision who are going through just exactly what I went through with no early intervention and prevention.

Why do they have to wait and go through many years of pain and misery and end up in an institution before they are offered help or become another statistic of premature death through adverse childhood experiences (ACEs) as when I reflect back to school days I always sat at the back of the class with others like me. Where are those guys today? in addiction centres? in prison? only a couple that I can think about including myself -because the rest are DEAD.

I done the courses that were offered and a lot more. I had a reason to live; I had a purpose. I got my early release with my extension added. I left prison still in addiction and managed to get into a residential rehab where for the first time in thirty years, I got clean. I was bursting with life.

I did a lot of work on myself from the inside out to discover that no one was to blame for where I ended up and what had happened. People places circumstances captained my ship and became the master of my fate ran me aground many times in the CJs and prison or let me adrift in an ocean of addiction.

Me and a couple of other guys with past lived experience started up a charity called Aid & Abet. We go into prisons all around Scotland supporting prisoners before there release then pick them up at the gate on the morning of their release. Get them housed sort there benefits and GP. Then look at where else we can help them help themselves., Into training employment, and some cases into rehab and on to a better way of living.

These guys are broken adults like myself, Broken, busted, disgusted, and could not be trusted.
We try to fix broken people. We are all volunteer's living of £3 meal deals out the shops and using concession bus passes to get around. We are doing an amazing job, and

people are talking about the success that we are having and most importantly, we are doing it from the heart.

One day I get a phone call from the police. "Hello, Kevin, it's the police" "Aye what is it" You see the last time I spoke to the police on the phone they had surrounded my house with guns to shoot me. But today I'm trying to do relationships. The police go on to say. "Kevin we hear what you're doing in Edinburgh and the Lothian's with Aid & Abet we find it very interesting as we are doing a similar project would you mind coming in to see us.

I go and meet up with these cops, four of them who are doing something similar with 16 to 25-year-olds. What I see is cops with compassion! Who are getting these young men and women away from crime and drug addiction and into training and employment. Early intervention and prevention before they become statistics to premature death.

The problem the cops had was that they are cops! The "us and them" barriers were up, and when they approached a lot of these guys, a majority would kindly tell them to fuck off! "Yir the fuckin police". But they did have success but felt they could do a lot better if I Joined them with one of my colleagues from Aid &Abet. Using our lived experience and help prevent these young adults from becoming broken adults.

Of course, I want to be part of this prevention and early intervention!

"Cops & Cons" "working together to prevent these young adults becoming broken adults! What an opportunity! what a gift , to be able to get to these young people who have experienced Ace's (adverse childhood experiences) on the periphery of organised crime and drug addiction.

Now I work daily out in the car with the cop's helping young people into training, employment, housing and other needs to help them move on to a more positive destination.

Looking back at the day when my house is surrounded by armed police walking down the path, looking down to see red dots on my chest getting eye contact with the cops' marksman. I see his face every day;

every day, I see his face. Not in my mind, No! In the office, I work with him today. The cop involved that day is my college, my friend, we do a fantastic job together.

Then I get another phone call to the VOW project (police Scotland) where I'm now seconded from Aid & Abet. It's from Edinburgh council Health and wellbeing. They are asking would I like to get involved in their new project TYLA (turn your life around). I'm thinking "wow"! I have turned my life around full circle and being asked to be involved in a project called Turn your life around (TYLA)

"What is turn your life around"? you may be asking? I work in schools today, I have been working with primary school kids, and even as I write this, I get emotional.

You see, I have a purpose today; I help these kids fulfill and chase their dreams not to be scared or full of fear due to circumstances out of their control. You see, that prison staff member who told me I would never work in schools. He was right at that time, with no purpose, no dream, no direction, of course, I would never work in schools.

I found my purpose and I help others find their dream and keep their dream and make sure they don't live my past nightmare. I'm supported when I go into schools by the police child phycologists, and it's all about relationships. Aid & Abet help broken adults. The vow project prevent young adults becoming broken adults. And to get into schools to get real early intervention and prevention will make a difference between premature death and kids chasing their dreams and achieving them.

I spent many years allowing people, places, circumstances, and no purpose no dream captain my ship and that became the master of my fate. Today I have a purpose I am the captain of my ship I am the master of my fate.

Kevin Neary

## Jessica

As a child, I knew to speak only when spoken to, and I tried, I really did, but I have always had too much to say myself. "No- one is interested in what you think", my father would remind me as my cheeks glowed from the embarrassment of yet another public scolding.

Being viewed favourably by others was extremely important to my parents, and I guess this was understandable given they were church ministers. My family, therefore, led a double-life where what happened behind closed doors remained hidden from the outside world.

At home, violent arguments would erupt, seemingly out of nothing. I hated it when my parents argued, and they argued a lot. My role, as I saw it, was to intervene. Mostly, my parents didn't take kindly to these 'interventions', and I would end up bearing the full force of their frustration, but at least it distracted them from arguing with each other.

My parents' work meant I moved schools frequently. Always 'the new kid with the funny accent', I wanted to fit in but did not know how. Consistently unpopular as I moved from school to school, I concluded there must be something fundamentally wrong with me.

As I stared at my reflection in the mirror, I saw a blonde-haired girl with brown eyes and a fringe. 'What is so wrong with me?' I wondered.

During my teenage years, I was adept at answering back; I reasoned I was going to 'get thumped anyway' so I might as well make it worth my while. By now, I understood my Mum's need for vast amounts of sleep and tranquillizers; ironic given my parents were managers of a unit for people with substance misuse difficulties.

I liked some of the residents, and they liked me. According to them, I was interesting, funny and attractive.
Attractive! I had always wanted to be attractive. At thirteen, I was unable to understand I was being groomed.

I was sixteen when my parents separated. Apparently 'staying together for the sake of the kids' hadn't worked. My mother had a new partner who 'wasn't really into kids', so I ended up in a homeless hostel. 'I'm not going to end up like the addicts in here' I told myself, though I quite enjoyed smoking cannabis with some of the residents.

I went to college and eventually became a student nurse. I was highly competent, but behind my uniform, I was an emotional wreck, drinking to oblivion most nights. I managed to hide my dependence on alcohol for a short time, but my alcohol problem soon became obvious to everyone except me.

One morning I found myself sobering up in a police cell. The criminal convictions I received, because of my drunken behaviour, brought my nursing career to an abrupt end.

After one of my alcohol-induced 'pity parties,' I severed the tendons in my wrist. The medical staff I had previously worked with treated my injuries. As humiliating as this was, it never occurred to me to stop drinking. If anyone dared challenge me about my drinking, I would argue criminal convictions (not alcohol) had screwed up my nursing career, and I'd had a bad childhood. That soon shut them up! I was much too caught up in self-centredness to care about the consequences to others of my drinking.

No-one starts out as a hopeless drunk, but that is how I ended up. I eventually became desperate enough to attend a support group. There I found an answer to my alcoholism; a relationship! Sick people attract sick people, and that was certainly true in my case. When this relationship failed to cure my addiction, I ended up homeless for a second time.

Exasperated by having to admit me for yet another detox, the doctors on the psychiatric ward added 'personality disorder' to my list of diagnoses. Incredulously, I agreed to attend a therapeutic unit and resolved to try the support group again, to see if I could find another boyfriend!

People tended to disapprove of my behaviour, particularly in groups, but nevertheless, support group members told me to 'keep coming back'. Somewhat puzzled, I did as they suggested. I suppose I must have attended one meeting too many because, much to my surprise,I finally started being honest about my drinking.
Through the meetings, I gradually learned it is okay to speak, to feel

and to trust, but most of all, I became useful. I discovered other people benefitted when I turned up sober; 'carrying the message' they called it.

After many years of therapy, I began to understand my parents as damaged people, who perhaps should not have been together. Today, I have the most wonderful relationship with them. I also found a way to forgive those who sexually abused me, which relieved of the resentment and self-pity that fueled my addiction.

As I made amends to those I had hurt, I found inner peace, and the compulsion to drink lifted.

I currently work for a mental health team in a men's prison and often hear stories like mine. During Auricular Acupuncture sessions, I tell prisoners they too can be free from the chains of addiction and use their experience to benefit others. My purpose in life is to carry this message. This is for three reasons:

1. To repay those who believed in me before I could believe in myself

2. It is a pleasure

3. It keeps me sober

Jessica X

These are very special people. I have come across real community power houses among them. I am equally in awe of every addict who has been to the gates of hell and recovered. I have been moved to tears hearing stories from people who are simply trying to make amends, and do the right thing.

The man who worked every hour to make sure his kids have the best of everything, and his acceptance that his past behaviour means that he is now unable to see them.

The elderly man who said he was sitting across from his wife who is now crippled with arthritis, wondering why she ever stayed with him, and realizing he didn't fulfill even one of her girlhood dreams. He resolves now to make her as comfortable as he can, making sure she has everything to make her life as good as it can be. That kind of raw honesty has brought me to tears.

The woman who carries a photograph of her adult daughter around, to remind herself that, in the grips of her addiction ,she tried desperately to abort her, and she keeps the photograph near to remind her how bad it was and how grateful she is now. Her humble ability to share that story to help others.

The women in prison who killed her husband in a blackout and had no memory of it, telling her story to help younger women.

The category A prisoners who, despite serving life sentences are creating a programme to discourage young men from gang culture.

My own sponsor Peter who had lost his teaching profession because of his alcoholism, and after leaving hospital after a long stay , took a position as an "Inspector of frying pan handles" ! For eight years he did that, while writing to every headmaster who was advertising a position, telling the truth about his past, until one Headmaster gave him a chance and he returned to teaching. He said he couldn't do anything about the children who he had let down through his drinking years, but he <u>could</u> make absolutely sure that all the children now in his care would get the best possible teaching he could provide. He taught many addicts too!

The man who turned up at the door of a woman he barely knew, with a box of groceries knowing she was struggling, because he said someone had done that for his family when he was in prison.

I have heard thousands of such stories, some quite heartbreaking, all inspiring, and make mine pale into insignificance. This kind of honesty and unconditional love is rare and precious and has taught me so much.

I aspire to stay among their numbers.

## Chapter Twelve
Sue's story.

___

After reading these messages from such wonderful people, I feel a bit presumptuous adding my own story! I am humbled to be in such company, but I owe it to them to contribute!

There's no doubt that my "story" is very similar to many others, and I am not sure that people want to hear about me! But mine is the only story I have any right to tell, and it is necessary for this book to make that contribution. It is certainly not because I am outstanding!

It is traditional when telling the story of our descent into addiction, and our recovery from it, to start with the bad stuff first! The recommendation is to show:

"What it was like" "What Happened" and "What it is like now".

Instead, I would like to overturn that tradition, and in the very spirit of hope and "Restoration", begin with a look at "What it is like now"!

I don't want to begin by lamenting my childhood's woes and the sordidness of my addictions, not that it isn't pertinent. However, in our book's spirit, I would like to explore how much of me has restored! And indeed how much further I need to go! Perhaps then I might look at "what it was like".

Today is my 73rd birthday! I had lots of lovely flowers and cards and messages, and I was very spoiled. It was beautiful, especially since I never really considered I would live beyond my thirties! The way I lived and abused myself should have dictated that.

Birthdays have a habit of making us reflect on things, and among other things, I have been thinking about my adopted mother, Eileen.

For the last twenty years of her life, she wandered around our little seaside town smiling and waving at people, she had a wealth of anecdotes (mostly exaggerated, and designed to show her brilliant wit or insight!)) and generally was seen as a "treasure". Little old ladies tend to bring out the protectiveness in people!

But what we see is never the whole picture. Few people heard the bitching, the judgmental comments, the religious bigotry, the unkindness that she and her sisters saved for behind closed doors.

It could be presumed that as she got older, she had "seen the 'light" and was busy making amends for past behaviour. And I hope that may be true; I think we all start to wonder about our past as we near the end of our lives. Nobody should pass up the chance of making honest change, or be denied the opportunity to "make amends".

But that doesn't alter the reality for those of us caught up in the "wake" she left behind! Most saw her as a charming "old lady". But she had a very dark side, that she kept hidden and was preserved for the "privileged" few! (I was the most privileged!)

I am talking about this not to sound off about her! With the compassionate insight I try and adopt these days, I understand that she was probably a product of her own distorted upbringing, that she had her "demons" to face.

No! this is to remind me as I am enjoying my flowers and kind messages, that I am now that "old lady" and should not forget there is a "wake" I left behind!

And I can create all that misery again if I choose to - all I have to do is think I have "cracked it", and pick up a drink or a drug!!

As I write this, I am a Grandmother, a mother of six beautiful, talented, funny, honourable children and three delightful grandchildren. I can't take any credit for them; I am afraid that anything I have learned about child-rearing I have discovered after they grew up! They are all quite remarkable, in their own right.

I have been many things in my journey, as well as a mother, a counsellor, a restaurant owner. I have worked in what seems like a million bars and restaurants, factories, shops, nursing, you name it! (once I was even a magician's assistant!). Still, as a qualified Traditional Acupuncturist, I have been treating patients with various conditions for 25 years.

It is the treatment and understanding of addiction, however, where my real passion lies.

I am the head of Smart-UK, (NOT to be confused with Smart-recovery which is a very different organisation!). I have personally taught over twenty thousand healthcare workers in the 24 years since we started. I sometimes have to pinch myself!

Over the years, of course, I was not alone. I had my great colleague and friend Dr Kim Wager at my side, sharing his knowledge and wisdom. This work is my driving passion and continues to excite me. As I delve further into it, learning more, I have innovated new arms to the organisation.

What started as a response to pleas from a psychiatrist I worked alongside, for more science-based teaching, in line with clinical governance, has now grown into the world's leading organisation teaching auricular acupuncture for substance misuse. Based on addiction's neuroscience, our programme is used in the NHS, all the major addiction charities, 128 UK prisons, and many mental health services.

To say I am proud of Smart-UK and the people we have taught would be an understatement. I could never have envisaged how it has grown into such a community, and where it has taken me. There have been huge barriers broken down. We've taught discipline prison officers, doctors, nurses, all manner of healthcare professionals, and we even have nuns doing this treatment in the night out of a van in a city centre for sex workers! That is a hell of a lot of barriers broken down!

As human beings, everything we learn has no doubt been informed by what we have previously learned. We adapt our understanding as it expands, if we didn't do so, we would all still believe the world us flat!

So my understanding of addiction has also changed and developed organically from our teaching, studies, and research. It has also enabled me to unravel a little of my own background, and make sense of my complicated brain wiring!

What I teach now has minimal bearing on what we taught twenty-four years ago. Our evolved and evolving understanding, along with personal experience, has informed this book.

Every time I hear of addiction being maligned, I experience something akin to a primal scream! It feels like a knife in my heart! It feels personal- after all, it could be me being misunderstood!

I believe that the negativity surrounding the addict is mostly misplaced and is, in fact, a hindrance to real "recovery."

It is scientific evidence and real education of the facts that hold the key.

In 2010 I was surprised and honoured to receive a "Lifetime's achievement award" for my contribution to addiction treatment. (I always think those things are usually reserved for when you are about to drop dead!) I was indeed surprised and honoured in equal measure, but in my acceptance speech, I said, quite truthfully, that it was a bit like giving someone a huge box of chocolates, and then an award for eating them!

Because I am passionate about this work, it is not a chore, and It continues to be my "Raison d'etre"!

More recently, I have created a specific training for "5-star Wellbeing coaches" for the prison population, which is going exceptionally well. It is now being adapted and can be beneficial to anyone, so I intend to expand it further in the next few years.

It has been exciting teaching the prisoners themselves about the brain and addiction and watching them embrace this new perspective, and in turn, start to pass that on to their peers.

In my other role, I am the co-founder of Survivors Voice - Europe, an international charitable organisation supporting survivors of catholic clergy abuse, along with my colleague and friend Ton Leerschool from the Netherlands. We are both survivors of catholic clergy abuse.

We have always felt that our contribution to that particular fight should support individual survivors, rather than just banner waving. Once again, *education* of the actual severity of childhood sexual abuse. *(The damage caused to the brain especially)*

That is "Empowerment"!

Never a day goes by when I do not think of childhood clergy abuse. Every single day! It is not that I particularly want to dwell on it; it is an unpleasant subject. I have no desire to re-victimise myself, and actually, my abuses are not the ones these days that I consider too much. But every single day I am told of yet another injustice, another damaged life, or another premature death. Another family in turmoil. Another priest is evading criminal justice, another cover-up, another whitewash. Another Guru who thinks he has the answer.

In my professional life too, and my studies, I learn more and more devastating facts about the severity of childhood abuse damage: the brain damage, the damage to the immune and other metabolic systems, the shortened life span.

So it is hard to keep it out of my mind. That, of course, has been the choice I have made. I decided to be active in this Universal fight, so I knew this would be the case.

The years that I was unable to talk about my abuse didn't take the daily thoughts away. The years after I was able to speak out still didn't take away these thoughts! So I had a choice: to be part of the fight or witness others fighting while still being haunted by it. Either way, I am going to have to think about it every single day.
I could not just sit and watch, so I have chosen to be part of the fight.

In that capacity, I have spoken at many rallies, been featured on television and radio, have spoken in the Italian and Polish parliament and contributed to a powerful TV documentary. I was instrumental in a successful charge against the Holy See, (The catholic church) with the UN's Committee for the rights of the child. Later, with the UN's Committee against torture, (because childhood sexual abuse is considered torture in the articles of the UN ) and the church was found to have breached several of the articles of the UN.
I made the first rallying speech against the pope's visit in 2010 to 20,000 supportive, wonderful people!

In 2014 I received "Inspirational Woman of the year" award. This time for Human Rights. (Another enormous surprise) .The abuse of children by the churches and others is most definitely a human rights violation. These awards have made me reflect on my life and who I am today.

I lost friends, patients, and even cousins because of talking openly about my abuses; there are those who cannot bear to have their entrenched beliefs threatened. That expectation of silence and compliance is how I lived as a child. I refuse to have my pain negated any longer.

I have been married to my wonderful second husband, Gez, for over thirty years. A true hero who took six kids on board and me! A grand passion, who is now my solid rock. I am, I know, very complex, and I am sure challenging to live with!
I have fourteen life-threatening or limiting conditions, and I am registered disabled, the blame for all of which I lay entirely at the feet of the catholic church.

We know from our research that Adverse Childhood Experiences (ACE" s) of which childhood clergy sexual abuse is a huge one, will put our lives on a different trajectory. It will also cause damage to our brains, immune and other systems and shorten our life span by about twenty years.

I would opine that anyone brought up in the oppressive catholic church has sustained damage, even without the clergy abuse. There is a tendency to laugh about "catholic A levels in guilt." But for those of us that lived through it, and have that burden of church induced guilt, it isn't that funny!

I have recovered from a most unsuitable adoption,(I was bought; actually, money changed hands, not sure how much!) A pernicious catholic indoctrination, clergy sexual abuse, alienation, alcoholism, addiction, self-harming, an eating disorder, a violent first marriage, attempted murder, and being a single parent of six children! It has certainly not been a smooth ride, but from where I came from, to where I am now is like a mammoth leap!

And I am absolutely not exceptional, I believe that any addict has powers beyond their wildest dreams, given the right understanding, education and opportunity.

I won't blow by blow into the depths of my addiction, it is pretty much the same as for most other addicts, denial and steady sordid descent into misery, for ourselves and those around us. Suffice to say I am well qualified to belong to that club! Mine is not an unusual story, but it is the only one I have the right to tell.

I always knew there was something very different about my use of alcohol and other chemicals. I didn't know what that was, I didn't have the language, but I did see clearly that it was different from those around me. I had that genetic predisposition that we talked about earlier, unknown to me then.

I always felt like a square peg in a round hole; I hear many adopted people feel this way. Even those whose adoption has been handled sensitively are left with the same "separation" anxieties. My adoption wasn't "handled with care", I felt like an alien from a very early age. Even though I wasn't ever told of my adoption, and later when I worked it out, I was not allowed to speak about it, I always felt like a "Cuckoo in the nest."

Later, it was clear that everything I struggled with, every foot I put wrong had been put down to something they referred to as "throwback"! Everything I did right was considered to be as a result of my adoptive parent's benevolence! I realised that my mother thought she deserved infinite credit for adopting me.

I discovered alcohol at a very young age, maybe ten or eleven, and I thought the stuff had been made for me! It immediately made me feel better, braver, less afraid. *(I always thought that I was fundamentally flawed, and of little consequence, in fact, I felt sacrificial.)*

I took to booze like a duck to water! I sought alcohol at every opportunity. Luckily my adopted family were very "alcohol oriented", it seemed it was a panacea for all ills. You were given whiskey for a bad chest, brandy for a stomach upset, gin for what was referred to as" female troubles", a raw egg in sherry as a tonic, and Buckfast tonic wine which was reputedly suitable for everything having been made by monks! Copious amounts of cigarettes accompanied all of those. (I was allowed to smoke openly at the age of eleven!)

So it was relatively easy for me to get hold of alcohol! By the time I was fifteen, I was already a drinking alcoholic, playing truant from school or behaving in a grossly bizarre fashion, (too many strange habits to mention!) was having blackouts, and often didn't know where I had been or with whom. I was covered in self-inflicted and infected scars. I kept them as open sores and infected intentionally. **I was mentally and emotionally disturbed. In this day and age, I would probably have been locked up!**

We lived on the East coast, and there were five of us. My adopted Mother, Father and two spinster maternal aunts (seven more maternal Aunts lived elsewhere but visited regularly!). It was very much a female-dominated household, and they were tightly bonded siblings.

My mother, Eileen, was the youngest sibling, and always the centre of attention. She was quite theatrical, a beautiful singer. She played the piano (and, inevitably, the organ at church) She was, I am sure, a frustrated actress, and should have been on the stage. She compensated for not being in the theatre by "acting" all the time and performing for everyone she came into contact with.

She was a perpetual actress, and you could never know who she was. Nor could you ever believe what she said! She would "embroider" everything. She was also often very ill, so we all had to spend hours praying for her, having "masses" said for her, or visiting her in the hospital. She was doted on by the "sainted spinster aunts", for whom she was a surrogate baby (and I became her dolly). It was a bizarre household!

My Father Lewis was an incredibly kind man, I feel that had he lived, my life might have been different, but he died of a brain tumour when I was twelve. Even that frightening experience was trivialised! My dad's death was broken to me by one of the Aunts handing me a glass of whiskey and a lit cigarette, saying "Your Daddy's happy" I then was expected <u>Not</u> to cry; otherwise I would have shown a distinct lack of faith.

The sisters doted on Eileen even more after she became widowed, and I had three "mothers"to please, all with their own outdated and bigoted opinions on how I should behave!

I was never allowed to ask about my origins. Eileen would be furious, offended, and even cruel if the subject were broached. She did a beautiful line in emotional blackmail! When aged 22, I forced the "adoption" conversation, much to her annoyance, she gave me a variety of "embroidered" stories about my birth, all different, depending on her mood!.

She had a distinct cruel streak, but she was indeed charismatic, and I guess I loved her; for she was all I knew. I try and adopt compassionate hindsight these days. I think she was also a product of her distorted catholic upbringing and must have had her disappointments, and pain.

When talking to me, I don't think she ever said anything that wasn't hideously "passive-aggressive"! *"Everyone is watching you, and everything you do comes back on me!"* *"And worse than that -everyone KNOWS you are a catholic"!* was a constant cry. She and the Aunts would stop talking to me regularly and for weeks on end  for minor transgressions.

She may well have thought that adopting a child would give her some fulfillment, perhaps the public completeness she craved. She gave the impression that she adopted me, and my Father was just a bystander. I certainly felt like her "doll", seen and not heard" preferably.

Initially, my name had been Christine, but there was another cousin called Christine, so they changed mine. I kept Christine as a second name. Bizarrely, I always thought of myself as Christine when I was a child, and once I even said I preferred it. After that, Eileen wouldn't speak to me for ages, so I never brought it up again. My mother had a PhD. in guilt inducement as well as emotional blackmail! *(When my first granddaughter was born, my daughter Louise called her "Christina". She had been so incensed by the idea of my having my name taken off me that she wanted to "claim" it back!)*

In my forties, I did discover my birth origins and met some blood relations! My birth mother had died twelve years previously, but had sisters alive and five other children! There was a meeting arranged, and although they were charming people, they were absolute strangers, we had no shared history, or anything much in common, I didn't know how to be a sister, and it never went any further.

Our entire lives revolved around the catholic church and its calendar, and our home was a "shrine" in itself. There were statues and holy pictures all over every room in the house: There were superstitions and signs from god everywhere you looked, although I was never "worthy" enough to see them! catholic clergy were to be revered; they were considered next to god and could do no wrong. I must always remember that it was a "blessing" every time a priest crossed your doorstep.

The family had a strange attitude to suffering; any pain I experienced was considered something to be "grateful" for. We should *"offer it up"* in atonement for our many, "sins", both past and future. Sympathy ought never to be sought; it was very much a dirty word!

"You are gasping for breath? "(I am asthmatic) – *"Offer it up"*! "You have a broken foot? "(I fell off a swing) – *"Offer it up"*!

"You are sick? You have measles?-whooping cough?-pneumonia?" *"Offer it up"*!

It seemed that any physical pain I went through was of no other consequence than to be used as an offering! I was shamed into thinking that I was selfish for crying or complaining about pain. I should use my mother as an example, she and her sisters said, for despite being always so ill, she welcomed her pain, so she got the chance to *"offer it up"*! I still have a sense that felt any pain I suffer is of little consequence.

Their constant mantra, when I put a foot wrong or questioned anything was "OBEDIENCE" with emphasis on the "O" It seemed that disobedience of any kind was the worst "sin". They were entirely oblivious to anyone's emotional suffering any emotional pain.Any mental turmoil, would have been considered "lack of faith."

We spent hours and hours at church! We were to starve in Lent, Celebrate at Easter, attend May processions. Observe" Holydays of Obligation", say the Rosary at bedtime, attend "Catechism classes", Benediction, Stations of the Cross. No meat on Friday, Fast days, Weekly confession, Venial sins, Mortal sins, Sins of omission...it seemed that everything apart from breathing was sinful and warranted punishment of some kind.

I was asthmatic and had suffered from Whooping cough just before the 1953 floods on the East coast. Being caught up in that flood had resulted in pneumonia (the legacy from which has been chronic Asthma and Bronchiectasis). But aged six years old, all I knew was that I hated the cold, and it affected my breathing. (*"Offer it up!!"*)

I had to go weekly to confession, from the age of six, where we told all of our "sins" to the priest behind a somewhat inadequate grill. The confession was an embarrassing affair, even for children of that age. We knew that the priest knew precisely who we were. ( I consider the entire practice of confession to be child abuse.)

Through all of those early years, I honestly expected to become a martyr! Not the kind of "terminal doormat", who whinge a lot and we all tend to cringe at, but a real "suffer intolerable torture and die for your faith" kind of martyr. I was told that there might come a time when I would have to die for my "faith".I was never told why that might be, but it was further fear-inducing.

When I was about six, my mother and her sisters made me kneel with them and pray for an older cousin to die. He was about to marry a divorcee with two children and his mother, my aunt, was told by her parish priest that she should pray for him to have a "happy death" that it was far better for him to die than to embark upon a life of sin.

As I knelt with them, I trembled at the thought of ever doing anything that deserved such punishment. I was quite sure that every time I committed a "sin" someone, somewhere was praying for me to die. I began to believe that I deserved to die! I began to hate myself, to feel completely insignificant, and that legacy has never entirely gone away, much to my husband's frustration!

My adopted family was fiercely superstitious, judgmental and pious in a time when these sorts of Catholics saw themselves as a persecuted minority.

When a priest sexually abused me from the age of ten until I was 13, and because of the family's "priest obsession", I could never talk about it. For a long time, I was even able to lie about it rather than letting anyone know. I was so sure it was my fault. Priests could do no wrong, so I must be evil, and the cause of what happened.

When my mother actually caught him in "the act", when I was thirteen, she did nothing about it! She told me to "pray for him"! And "offer it up"!! She said that it must be part of "God's plan"! I didn't think it was a very good one.

She refused to speak about it again and continued with her priest sycophancy, and I felt sacrificial. After that, I had absolutely no one to turn to, I had no trust in anyone or anything, and I became a disturbed and rebellious mess.

My drinking increased, along with all the misery that it brought, I would try any mind-altering chemical, I honestly thought I was a hopeless case. I was frequently and seriously suicidal, riddled with guilt and shame. It is perverse that children who are abused in this way have such a profound sense of guilt when the blame is not theirs.

My life was spiralling downwards, and I couldn't stop it.

Mine wasn't a story I could share with other girls, not a story for around the Brownie campfire, or in giggling sleepovers. I became a chameleon, keeping secrets and hiding behind a disturbed and chaotic persona. I was on a massive downward spiral, my life having been put on a different trajectory.

I even preferred to be poorly thought of, rather than show my pain. I became a perpetual "blame acceptor".

I was married at seventeen (to get away from home) to someone quite immature and inadequate. It was like going from the frying pan into the fire! I was equally inept, an alcoholic and emotionally disturbed, playing at being a grown-up, and so the whole thing was a disaster in the making.

As my drinking got worse, so did the constant violence, until it became a sickly vicious circle. We moved around the country, usually to avoid the debts that had built up, and I didn't feel anywhere was home. Nor was I able to make my children feel secure.

Incredibly, though, I had a feeling that somewhere deep inside me there was something worth saving, a sort of a "green shoot" of something decent, desperately trying to force it's way up. A bit like a blade of grass desperately trying to push it's way up through something as hard as concrete. Once again, I didn't know what to call it; I just *felt* it.

It took me until I was twenty-nine before I was able to do anything about it. By that time, I had six children, was in a disastrous violent marriage and had no money or support, no family network, and was drinking daily. It felt utterly hopeless.

I had heard people talk about "spiritual awakenings" a sort of burning bush moment when everything changed. Usually, those things come about when things are at their very worst when there has been a tragedy or shameful event that prompted them to seek help. I have heard many horror stories in sobriety from people who had the most dreadful "rock bottoms".

I can't pretend I had anything at all of that nature., In fact, when I did stop; it was not at a time when my drinking was at its height, worse things had occurred many times before. I had plenty of "rock bottoms", and I had got out of many hideous scrapes by the skin of my teeth.

What I did have, though, was a desperate love for my children, despite all of my inadequacies. My ex-husband and I should never have been together, certainly shouldn't have had children together; we were not sane, responsible adults. But we did have them, I am privileged to have them, and I love them more than my life.

Aged 29, I had what can only be described as "a moment of clarity" when I saw quite clearly that if I didn't do something about this NOW, then there would be a tragedy in my home, that may very well involve my children, and, after my own miserable childhood, that thought was more than I could bear.

I had to find a solution; I knew I needed help, but couldn't imagine many people that could help. I was never good with people. I was terminally mistrustful, and had a belligerent attitude which was mostly my survival "armour". (It is often still there!!)

For most of my teenage and adult life, I had been looking for a place to belong, I had always felt an intense "homesickness", although for what exactly, I couldn't say. Some people, I concluded, are just meant to be on the "outside"!

I always envied people who knew exactly who they were, where they came from, were connected to others and knew where they fitted into the grand scheme. I was, and still am, in awe of family "history" and long-held traditions. Over the years I have tried to "belong" to so many different groups, but of course, you cannot belong to something to which you don't belong!

My upbringing and my abuses as a child made me alienated from society most cruelly. Having to keep dark secrets and not having anyone to talk to about them furthered my sense of isolation.
Fear of a god, of retribution, and the poisonous indoctrination of the catholic church kept me powerless and further subjugated me. I not only didn't know who I was, but I didn't even know <u>what</u> I was! I always felt like a square peg in a round hole.

Booze was my crutch and medicine, and I became an ALIEN in the world to which I so badly wanted to belong.

I didn't belong in the family - but I couldn't function outside of the one into which I had been thrown.

I didn't belong in the church, I had no belief in god,(although I was afraid to admit that) and because of abject fear, I couldn't get out of the church. (until much later)

I became a permanent "outsider". That pattern has continued for the whole of my life, being a spectator of many things, but never totally belonging, an alien impersonating a human being.

But then came this time aged 29 when I did find REAL honest human beings!

When I had that moment of clarity aged 29, I picked up the phone and asked Alcoholics Anonymous for help. It saved my life (and by extension, my children's lives).

I had heard of AA from a previous neighbour, and although I didn't know much about it, it seemed at the time that it was the only option. The person who answered the phone to me that night, Peter S, saved my life, he took me under his wing and introduced me to a new and sober lifestyle that I could never have envisaged. I began going to AA meetings and learn about a new way of life and NOT drinking!

My disastrous marriage didn't last very much longer after that. I was no longer easy to manipulate, I was less malleable, I was taking responsibility, and I had supportive people around me for the first time. So after a last-ditch attempt to bump me off,(by feeding me with benzodiazepines when I was half asleep!) my ex-husband walked out and "sailed off into the sunset"!

It was the best thing that could have happened, there ceased to be a toxic environment in my home, but it did leave me with six children under twelve, with no support whatsoever, and under threat of eviction! He rarely paid any child maintenance, and when he was forced into a corner, it was woefully inadequate.

He has never sent any of my children a birthday card or a present; he never acknowledged their incredible achievements, (they all have good degrees and professions) he has never met his grandchildren.

My kids and I gathered a shield around ourselves, and it became "them and me" against the world!. We were rehoused in a grotty area, but kept ourselves to ourselves and were soon rehoused int a more pleasant one. I got a job, then a better job learned to drive, got a car, then went back to college, studied hard and got a profession.

AA is not a magic bullet, of course, there is hard work involved, and It wasn't easy learning to navigate this new way of being. Still, gradually as the "onion skins" were peeled back and my eyes were beginning to open, I could, at last, see a glimpse of a healthy future. I could also recognise the toxicity of my past. My children were thriving, I was working, and all was much better.

Peter became my sponsor, a close friend, and the most significant influence in my life. An honorary grandfather to my younger children. He held my hand metaphorically through my early sobriety, as I got stronger, and 15 years later, I was privileged to hold his as he died.

After I met my wonderful husband, Gez, I was embarking on a new life, and we were finding our way through the garbage of my life when absolute disaster almost destroyed us.

My oldest son Nick was killed in a car crash; he was just 19. I was devastated, as were my other children; we had been such a close bunch, and to lose one of us was like a limb being torn off. I doubted I would ever recover. It was only with their love, along with love from Gez and my AA friends that I survived. I remain thankful daily for these people!

My mother didn't come to Nick's funeral, she claimed to be unwell, but later a cousin told me that she said that god had decided Nick should be killed to spare him from "going off the rails". What kind of god would that be?? Perhaps she thought I should "offer it up"! I am sure she also said it was in retribution for my marrying outside of the church, and she was undoubtedly praying for me to die!

I have never been able to forgive her. Even when my heart was utterly broken, my pain and that of my other children was insignificant. I cannot even write this sentence without crying.

I saw this poisonous religion for what it was. One of my biggest regrets is the many years of my time wasted being in that cult. One incredible legacy that my son left me was, despite my heartbreak at losing him, at last, the ability to get away from that church and be free of the shackles of indoctrination.

My AA friends and my family held me up when I wasn't able to stand alone. There was, and still is, a lot I don't resonate entirely with about AA, the dependence on a "Higher power", I am an Atheist (albeit a sort of Buddhist one!). The constant references to "shortcomings" and "defects of character". I already felt absolutely worthless. I didn't need that constant reminder!

With my knowledge of how the brain works, I understand now that to perpetuate something in this negative way, going over and over it, makes it more robust,(Long term potentiation) and I want that part of me diminished.

Neither can AA see any kind of "graduation" and suggests one will always be "in recovery" and powerless. I appreciate the humility in that, but I do disagree with the powerlessness.

There is a great reluctance in AA to let go of 1930's thinking, despite current research. That overall belief in being at the mercy of a "higher power`" I refute the idea of a celestial puppet master deciding my fate. It can have an unfortunate "cult-like "characteristic to it.

However, there is no doubt the **people** in AA have saved many lives, including mine, it is where I began, and I have immense gratitude for them being there. I still love being in their company when I can. My rule of thumb with everything, including Chinese medicine, AA, and life in general, is to take out of it, and embrace that which is valuable and leave behind that which is not. Being at last able to discriminate is a gift.

There are many valuable truths I do share with AA. The absolute necessity for abstinence, the need to make amends, remove triggers, and the knowledge that it is not possible to "go back". Trying to live "a day at a time" do "The next right thing", and stay in the moment has saved my sanity on many occasions!

For me, though, having always felt like an "alien", it has been the "fellowship", that was a revelation. It is a human imperative to be connected to a tribe, pack, family etc. So here, among drunks and junkies, dukes and dustmen, with their humour, honesty, humility, compassion, lack of judgment, and unconditional love, *I had, at last, found a tribe!*

These days that tribe has grown to include many different circles. Some very special people, not only my family and AA/NA but my students, my patients, my colleagues. People I respect and have taught me so much. Some in recovery who have also become beacons of truth and hope, many are in different countries, and some are in prison!

I am often told that I have forged a "good life" and that now in my later years I am "O.K.", and indeed that is true. But my early years and teens and twenties were lost, and cannot be reclaimed. I wasn't free to grow and develop skills naturally; I was too busy trying to survive!

I was permanently in "Fight or Flight" mode, perpetually hyper-vigilant! My life has been like driving like fury in a car with only three wheels, never quite straight, always a little bit wonky, rickety and never quite smooth or on track! Still speeding away though, but ever the alien!

I now have, at last realised that being an "alien" can be O.K! Being on the "outside", on the sidelines is not necessarily such a bad place to be! I can't "belong" in the same way as others, but it is O.K. As Spike Milligan famously once said "Everybody has to be somewhere!" and this is where I am!

I have learned that diversity is essential, the Universe needs different peoples with different experiences and different skills in its population, and that each one of us has a part to play.

Being a little outside of things can be quite useful, it means that sometimes I can help, without having to get involved with negative politics, and other peoples issues. *(I still feel the need to protect myself and my vulnerabilities)*

It means too that sometimes I have a view of things not afforded to those on the "inside."

It means that sometimes I can be instrumental in many different areas, perhaps in a small way, rather than being valid in only one place.

It means that sometimes I can be a bridge from one world to another.

It means that I can be a small part of many things, rather than a big part of a little something.

It means that I can be a small part of a lot of people's lives and have many people each being a small part of mine.

It means that I can sometimes see the broader picture instead of being bogged down with the immediate crisis.

Working in a professional capacity in addiction treatment has helped me play a part in that world, and being an addict means I am accepted by those still battling their demons. These are things for which I am truly grateful.

Having the ability to function a little in a lot of areas aren't attributes, these are things that have come about through my adversity and alienation, and which have allowed me to survive. It means that I can make a contribution!

*And this has been it!*

Sue Cox

*I was listening to the radio a while back when I heard an autistic boy saying that the first time he could "justify his existence" was when he started to connect with trees and animals.

I had to go even further, right back to the Big Bang. When the atoms that made me were first formed. The fact that I am made of stardust really resonates with me, given that my default mindset is still that of unworthiness and self-loathing! Physics tells me that despite my background and addictions, and my default feeling of insignificance, it is the same stardust that makes me up like every other living thing, and is equally as important.*

A Final Thought from my friend the wonderful anthropology
Professor David Orenstein from New York University.

Dr. David I. Orenstein
Professor of Anthropology Medgar Evers College/CUNY

The world needs you. The world needs all of us. How we make the leap
from the one to the other is a case for cultural synaptic movement. This
physical movement is at once electric as it is deeply personal and based
on the construct of our experiences. Much in the same way our brains
fire to recognize love, pain, pleasure, and memory. One can make the
argument that when we are in personal stress or under psychological
duress it is clearly impossible for us to honestly connect to our feelings
of joy and empathy. If we cannot connect to our own singularity it is
equally impossible to connect then to the joy and suffering of others.

The relatively new field of neuroscience is bursting at the seams with
deeply important research that helps scientists, clinicians and citizens
alike to know more about how our gray matter works. How our brains
define and control our experiences. How the universe within our heads,
the place once believed to be the holding place of the soul, is now in
modernity acknowledged to serve as the material space that represents
all of our reality. From before our birth until to the day we die it is our
brain, this evolved ganglia of soft tissue, which itself cannot feel
pleasure or pain, that will define all our emotions, perceptions and
experience.

If you are reading this book, you probably already know that there are
so many internal and external forces that can impact our brains. The
research shows that in gestation, as our brain chemically develops, it is
forming the necessary pre-wiring for our future selves. Everything from
our innate ability to suck, to the chemical formation which controls our
gender identity happens before our birth. This chemistry will play a role

in less controversial aspects of our development, such as our "handedness," and it will eventually play an even greater part in the social calculation of who we become as adults.

Whether we become a mathematician or soccer player, a dancer or electrician, an anthropologist or social worker, is impacted primarily by our fetal development and secondarily but equally importantly by how we are nurtured throughout our formative and adult years.

Once out of the womb, it is primarily the human lottery system of place of birth and to whom we are born which will generally set the course of our mental and emotional lives. Such randomness impacts brain development and puts us all on the road to our opinions, values, expectations, experiences, educational attainment, social class, language, as well as our ethnic and cultural identity.

To complicate matters further, overlay this birth lottery with the possibilities of organic illness, genes gone wild, and accidental or purposeful brain injury. All of these variables, when taken holistically, lead to almost immeasurable possible outcomes related to brain health and mental illness, addiction and recovery, and overall personal wellness.

This all leads to one fundamental and for some, a startling conclusion. What neuroscience, sociology, medicine and anthropology have clearly shown is that free will is an illusion. Such a concept, used to define divine providence, or at least divine intervention in the course of human action, simply does not exist. There is no human life that is a self-fulfilling prophecy. Once we begin to think this way, we stratify by good and bad, we offer less hope, access and care to those in need and greater options and access to those who may not need the material wealth.

Clearly, we can mix these and so many social attributes and aspirations, just as it is clear that we can, under the right circumstances, alter our psychosocial and chemical states and thus our destiny and fate. Such is the pretext and the claims of this deeply insightful and valuable book.

Long held ideas of shame and even emotional violence against a person suffering from addiction are rampant in our history and the lay views of everyday people, in past ways we cared for the sick and the overall social pressure embedded in the assumption that the individual can, through the for of their will alone, conquer their "demons." But addiction is not about one's character. Addiction is indeed a chronic brain disorder and one which demands resources to education and intervene, experts in palliative care, an assurance that social stigma will not harm the individual, and a legal system which will not further damage a person lost within the pain of their disease.

We also know that there is a finely explored cycle of addictive abuse and the clinical stages are each well documented. From entry to initial use, through daily abuse, each leads the addicted individual down a path of ongoing suffering. The body's growing tolerance for the mental or physical substance always requires a more potent "hit" to reach the same high. Then the growing dependence on the substance or substances of choice and the potential for relapse, can lead to an endless cycle of addiction. This cycle not only disrupts the addictive person's life and saps them of their potential, but their addiction touches everyone they know and love.

Where does the pscycho-social meet the chemical construct of our brain chemistry with regard to addition? There are indeed many battlefields. Certainly ongoing poverty and a lack of access to healthcare resources is a glide path to dependency. But family history, victimhood because of abuse or neglect, violent or unstable living conditions, access to substances through those around each serves to cradle and foster abuse and addiction as well. If we include depression, other forms of mental illness and even loneliness, then the desperation of living within the confines of the stress of one's daily life may very well lead us to escape into the world of substance abuse.

Addiction also may even be considered an ancient biological response
to the environmental stresses of life. An adaptation that may have had
greater value earlier in our evolutionary history but is vastly counter-
productive and seen as dysfunctional now. In a 2010 paper written by
John Shelley-Tremblay and Lee Rosen, they explored the potential
evolutionary purpose of another gene-based adaptation seen as
maladaptive in our contemporary society. Upon looking at attention-
deficit hyper-activity disorder (ADHD), the authors noted that the
disease is genomic in nature and has its antecedence in our ancient
history.

In an even more recent study, Vanderbilt University geneticist Dr.
Anthony Capra synthesized Neanderthal DNA and found genetic
markers for the pretense of both depression and tobacco addiction. The
study stopped short of any predictive conclusions but did suggest that
the markers, while not predictive of behavior, could have served an
evolutionary purpose in the Pleistocene ecology of our distant past
relatives.  Dr. Capra notes, "In today's world, the (Neanderthal) genetic
legacy is either neutral or mildly harmful. So for people of Eurasian
ancestry, at least today, Neanderthal interbreeding was not so good to
us."

In 2016, Dr. Laura Weyrich, an evolutionary biologist from the
University of Adelaide, began studying the enzymes found on the
fossilized teeth of European Neanderthals. In her research, she found
that our hominid cousins used homeopathic remedies to sooth illness.
They used what we'd commonly refer to as folk substances to relieve
the pain of tooth and stomach distress. It should come as no surprise
that several of the specimens had a greater prevalence of substances on
their teeth than others. This can lead us to two conclusions; one is that
these individuals were sicker than their compatriots, and the second is
that they ingested more to get the benefits of the "high" even without an
associated pain or illness.

How cultures deal with biologically based addiction as well as other
western referenced genetic maladies vary within and between social
groups. In his landmark 1967 study of schizophrenia and first-nation
peoples, the anthropologist Julian Silverman suggested the following
functionalist perspective:

"Acute schizophrenic behaviors in our culture and    shaman
inspiration-gathering behaviors of certain primitive cultures are
considered in terms of several core psychological factors. Significant
differences between acute schizophrenics and shamans
are not found in the sequence of underlying  psychological events that
define their abnormal  experiences. One major difference is emphasized
—a difference in the degree of cultural acceptance of a unique
resolution of a basic life crisis. In primitive  cultures in which such a
unique life crisis resolution is tolerated, the abnormal experience
(shamanism) is typically beneficial to the individual, cognitively and
        affectively; he is regarded as one with expanded
consciousness. In a culture that does not provide referential guides for
comprehending this kind of crisis experience, the
individual (schizophrenic) typically undergoes an intensification of his
suffering over and above his original anxieties."

What Silverman had suggested and what has long been debated is that
in the absence of greater knowledge, those who could not describe or
even fathom that such illness could exist adapted mental illness. Indeed,
the social adaptation was not to make the schizophrenic an outlier, but
to give them great wealth, social importance and respect. The culture
grew to see what we would consider mental illness not as a malady but
as strength. Seeing those afflicted as holy men rather than turning them
into homeless men.

Such observation often plays out in own modern culture and
conventional wisdom. For instance, there's an old adage, "if 1,000
people believe you can hear the voice of god you become a prophet, if
no one believes the voices you're hearing are god you become a

patient." Perhaps we evolved this sensitivity to recognize mental illness in our modern culture.

If so, then recognizing addiction as a form of mental illness works to solve the pain and suffering of others regardless of any genetic predisposition or inheritance from Neanderthals and more recently our parents. So regardless of biological determinacies or social construct, helping those suffering though their addiction leads each of us to be a catalyst for those in pain. Placing their very well being under our individual and collective care. Even if the person is ungrateful for the support, no matter if the person suffering sees intervention (and you) and unwarranted, often times we are one another's last best hope.

While I am frequently not in favor in telling people what to think or how they should think, I believe we should and must laude the authors of this book. They have done their due diligence, they are survivors and practitioners. They are activists as much as they are humanists working to help those who are abandoned, ignored, dehumanized and forgotten.

To tell the tale of one's own tragedy and second chance is deeply moving. The stories and experiences collected in this work will indeed move you. Perhaps they will lead you seek treatment. Perhaps that will encourage and activate you to help others? In either case, from cover to cover, when this book is consumed by the eyes and the mind, you will not be the same person ever again.

While that may seem disturbing, I urge you to give this book a chance. You'll simply be more human when you're done reading it.

My thanks to Professor David Orenstein who is my dear friend, and a wonderful Humanist and Human being. He has promised to officiate at my funeral I hope to see him lots before then!

Suggested reading : I am not going to recommend a load of addiction books, there are millions! From the beginning we have talked about there being endless opinions! We all will each gravitate to the books and thoughts that we resonate with, they will be the right ones for us, and we will soon tire of the ones that aren't.There are loads out there! Look them up.

I do love these though!

Man's search for meaning          -          Victor Frankl

Humankind          -          Rutger Bregman

The Miracle of Mindfulness          -          Thich That Hanh

The Art of happiness          -          Dalai Lama

Godless Grace          -          David Orenstein

The Subtle art of not giving a f-ck          -          Mark Manson

The Human Being Diet          -          Petronella Ravenshear

One Step Beyond          -          Chris Moon

and I could not miss this one out!

Auricular Acupuncture and Addiction          -          Kim Wager with Sue Cox

There is no "index" page but a few reminders,

I have talked about being "Empowered" and indeed that is what I encourage people to be. Don't be manipulated. You will need a team, but pick them wisely.

If you want to try the twelve step programme it can be found worldwide. Easy access via phone book internet etc.The twelve step movement will tell you about abstinence, so in that respect it is very much in line with our thinking. But it is not for everyone so if you really don't resonate with the idea, don't beat yourself up!
Be careful of any services that think they can "reverse" Long term potentiation!

There are free substance misuse services in most towns in the UK, and many of them are doing a good ob. Some, however, are more concerned with the preservation of their service and less with the client, and sometimes they are ill equipped to deal with this issue. .These charities are effectively businesses, and they have to fulfill "targets" to receive their funding.so check them out! You do not have to have second best!There can be a "beggars can't be choosers" attitude that is simply unacceptable.

It will take some time to change the long held negativity that surrounds people living with addiction, but change it must!And you can help do that!

Only work with people who want the very BEST for you!(and understand what that is)Remember the Ten criteria we mentioned at the beginning, make sure you are happy that they are being met.

Be careful of services or therapists that makes claims that cannot be substantiated, evidence  is always best, there are a lot of purveyors of "snake oil" still!

If you want to try Traditional Acupuncture, make sure the practitioner is a member of the British Acupuncture Council and has the letters M. B.Ac.C  after their name, they should also have some understanding of addiction..

In "recovery," we often may  have to deal with historic issues like trauma, abuse  etc. In which case, there may be a few knots that you are unable to unravel on your own, and so you may want to seek therapy of some kind.

I am not going to recommend any specific one, but I would suggest that this is a rule of thumb when choosing one:

### Seeking Professional Help

It may be that you decide that you need to engage the services of a professional who can help you come to terms with change and support you as you move to find resolution in whatever form that means for you.

However it is very important that you hold out for the best quality therapy or counseling possible – this is important and intrinsic to your sense of self and future well-being and it needs to be handled in the best way possible for you, in the safest and most effective way.

Here are some basic tips on how best to find someone to offer support and help.

Firstly **YOU HAVE THE RIGHT TO CHOOSE!!!!**

At this point in the process you are going to be the customer in effect so you have the right to 'buy' precisely what you want.

So what is important to you about the person that you work with?

A good therapist, someone who is boundaried and ethical will appreciate and be OK with you asking lots of questions on the phone perhaps or with a pre-chat in person. If they are not OK with that then you might consider whether they are the right therapist for you – remember YOU CHOOSE.

We can only offer you an example of some of the questions that some people would like to know but feel free to add others Some of these may be important, some may not but they will give you an idea:
– How long have you been qualified?
– How long did it take you to qualify?
– Where did you qualify?
– What is your professional registration?
– What inspired you to become a therapist/counsellor?
– What professional body do you belong to?
– Can I have a copy of your ethical framework?
– Has any client ever made a complaint about you?
– Do you have experience of working with addiction/abuse/trauma?
– What is your model of therapy?
– How do you ensure that your spiritual/faith stance does not influence your work with clients?
– What is your position on clergy abuse?
– How much does this cost?
– How long do you envisage me being with you?
– How confidential are our sessions?
– Can you explain areas in our work where you may need to break confidentiality if any?
– What about notes – do you take them, do I have access to them, how secure are they?
– How sure can I be that you are fit for practice?
– Do you have supervision and how regularly?
– What happens if you are taken ill – what are the procedures for continuing therapy?
– What is the notice of cancellation of sessions?

There are probably lots more questions that might be worth considering, specific to your needs, but as a minimum these are a good starting point.

You have the right to check out credentials with the relevant professional bodies so you may like to ring up and verify qualifications.

If at any point during your initial conversation you feel uncomfortable, you are unhappy with an answer, you just don't feel that you connect with the therapist you can say that you will need to get back to them. YOU DO NOT NEED TO BE BULLIED INTO THERAPY!

It is not for everyone, but if you feel that you might benefit remember that you as the client are in charge of who you give your money to and MOST IMPORTANTLY: who you feel you can trust to respect and work with you in a way that suits you.

Remember you are going to be talking about some hard situations and it may not be quick to worth through – you should hold out for having a safe, non-judgmental, therapeutic relationship with your allocated healthcare professional – anything less is not good enough for you, what you are about to do is too important to settle for poor quality unethical practice.

If you have any doubts please do contact us whilst we cannot vouch for counsellors we can support you in finding someone to work with you.

---

# Remember you are made of Stardust! Take back your power and reach for the stars!

To contact us
www.suecox.website
suecox@smart-uk.com
info@smart-uk.com

You may not believe in magic,
But don't you think it strange,
The amount of matter in our Universe .
Has never slightly changed,
That all that makes your body,
Was once part of something more,
And every breath you ever breathe,
Has seen it all before
There are countless scores of beauty,
In all the things that you despise,
It could once have been a shooting star,
That now makes up your thighs,
And atoms of forgotten life,
Who've long since ceased to roam,
May now have the great honour,
To call your crooked smile their home,
You may not believe in magic,
But i thought that you should know,
The kings of your heart were born,
Fourteen billion years ago,
So next time you feel lonely,
When the world makes you feel small,
just remember that it's part of you,
And you're part of it all.

Erin Hanson

Lightning Source UK Ltd.
Milton Keynes UK
UKHW020851110321
380157UK00007B/48